DESIGN
THE GROUNDBREAKING MOMENTS

DESIGN
THE GROUNDBREAKING MOMENTS

NINA KOZEL
WITH CONTRIBUTIONS BY CLAUDIA HELLMANN

PRESTEL
Munich · London · New York

CONTENTS

"Design is everything— everything!" Paul Rand

INTRODUCTION

Design is omnipresent in our modern society. The cup from which we drink; the chair on which we sit; the clothes we wear; the automobile or airplane in which we travel—all these objects need someone to "give them a form." And the term has also acquired an adjectival form: we need think only of the *designer* sofa, the *designer* dress, and *designer* stereo equipment. But what, in fact, is design? What is hidden away behind this term, which is so heavily overworked nowadays?

"Design" is a relatively new English word that has become a worldwide export success like "industrialization," in the context of which it actually developed. Division of work led to the task of designing objects and then eventually to the need for a new term. Etymologically, "design" is derived from both the French *dessin* (drawing, pattern, plan, draft) and the Italian *disegno* (sign, drawing, sketch). The word appears for the first time in the Oxford English Dictionary in 1885, and is now defined as "a plan or drawing produced to show the look and function or workings of a building, garment, or other object before it is made." It is used not only for the process of designing but also for the resulting product. The English design critic Stephen Bayley has provided a short, apt definition of the meaning of design as it is used in this book: "Design is what happens when art encounters industry, when people begin to decide what products of mass production should look like." Basically, therefore, any object that has been planned, designed, and industrially produced is design.

With its 20 groundbreaking moments in design, this book is intended to provide an introduction to the development of modern design, from its beginnings in industrialization to the latest trends in product design. Both technical innovations and newly invented materials are presented, as are the various styles and cultural influences that have left their mark on design. At the same time, special objects and ideas that have had a lasting effect on the complex world of the design of everyday objects are presented. Design is a broad field subdivided into various subsidiary fields. The main focus of this book is the product design of exclusive consumer goods that reflect not only cultural and technical phenomena but also social developments.

1736–1819 James Watt   1796–1871 Michael Thonet

PIONEERS OF DESIGN: FROM CRAFTS TO INDUSTRIALIZATION

There was no such thing as a "designer" in pre-industrial society: utility objects were made by craftsmen and artisans and generally based on traditional forms. Although craftsmen could be creative and sometimes design things, until the advent of mass production it was not necessary to design objects in such a way that they could be produced serially. This had to be done by somebody who possessed not only a knowledge of the technical and material aspects of production, but also aesthetic design skills. This led to the creation of a new job at the interface of art and industry: the job of the designer, though they were not always called this in the past. There were numerous developments between the invention of the steam engine and the first industrially produced modern designs, even before the Bauhaus was established with the express aim of constituting the link between art and industry.

James Watt fired the starting pistol for the Industrial Revolution in 1775 when he developed an efficient steam engine, and in 1783 a rotary version

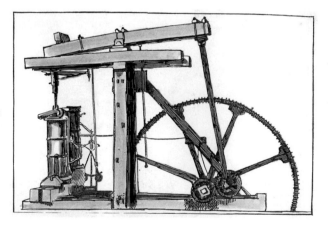

(fig. above), thereby providing an independent energy source for powering machines. A plethora of further technical innovations that would have an increasing impact on people's everyday lives soon followed. The period between 1830 and 1870 in particular is considered to have been the time of the "industrial take-off." This led to two decisive developments in the design of utility objects: firstly, design and production became separate from one another; and, secondly, an increasing number of objects and implement with new uses were invented, and these required appropriate designs.

left——CHARLES RENNIE MACKINTOSH, HILL HOUSE CHAIR | 1904
right——STEAM ENGINE BY JAMES WATT, 1788 | woodcut | 19th century

10/11 PIONEERS OF DESIGN ··· **1789–1799**—French Revolution ·· **1830**—Eugène Delacroix, *Liberty Leading the People* ············
1808—Johann Wolfgang von Goethe, *Faust* ···
1825—First public steam railway in England ···

Newly developed manufacturing methods made possible the speedy, inexpensive production of objects on a large scale. Aesthetic considerations, however, were not a priority. Untrained workers were often in charge of design, typically making machine-produced decorations that could then be attached to furniture, implements, and decorative objects. Whereas production made continuous progress, design remained nostalgic, imitating stylistic elements from the Renaissance, Baroque, and Gothic periods. An object's function was often obscured by exaggerated decorations, and even entirely new products were covered with historic ornamentation. Critics considered this to be an imitative and uncreative position. It resulted in a number of bizarre objects, such as a Renaissance-style sofa (fig. above)—bizarre because sofas did not appear until the nineteenth century, whereas the Renaissance flourished in the fifteenth and sixteenth centuries. This revivalism also reflected a desire for luxury items among the rising middle classes, who wanted to display their wealth and to emulate the aristocracy.

The achievements of the new age of the Industrial Revolution were presented to the public at the Great Exhibition in London in 1851, from new technologies, machines, and materials to industrially manufactured products. The greatest sources of excitement at the exhibition were the architecture of the vast exhibition hall, the newly constructed Crystal Palace by Joseph Paxton (fig. right), and the technology exhibited. But criticism of style was scathing: the great mass of things brought forth by the industrial age were said to be nothing more than copies of things from past ages, frequently of poor design and smothered in irrelevant decoration. William Morris, who with his reforming ideas would go on to breathe new life into art and

above——Renaissance-style triple back sofa | 19th century
right——Joseph Paxton, Crystal Palace for the Great Exhibition in London in 1851 | view of interior | c. 1900

TO THE
PICTURE
GALLERY

12 / 13 PIONEERS OF DESIGN ··· **1851**—Great Exhibition in London ···················· **1867**—Karl Marx, *Capital* ·················

·············· **1853–1870**—Georges-Eugène Haussmann's renovation of Paris ·················

···················· **1861–1865**—American Civil War ···················

1834–1896 William Morris   **1863–1957 Henry van de Velde**   **1868–1928 Charles Rennie Mackintosh**

William Morris's floral designs are considered an inspiration for Art Nouveau, his ideas and ideals the basis of modernism.

the crafts, described the exhibition quite simply as "wonderfully ugly." The first World's Fair thus played an important part in the early years of design: Britain, and also the rest of the world, was in a "style crisis" and had no choice but to recognize that quantity and price were not all that mattered. A number of counter-movements to revivalism developed in response to this state of affairs. In Britain, the most notable among these was the Arts and Crafts Movement that emerged around John Ruskin and William Morris. Both held capitalism and industrialization responsible for the ugliness of their time, and advocated drawing inspiration from the forms of working and living that had flourished in the Middle Ages. They wanted to improve the lives of people through good, simple designs. Whereas John Ruskin focused on the pursuit of socialist aims to improve the lives of workers in factories, Morris declared that his goal was to find an authentic style for the nineteenth century. In accordance with his ideals of simplicity and craftsmanship, and inspired by nature, he and his cooperative Morris, Marshall, Faulkner & Co. produced furniture and other decorative objects such as ceramics, wallpaper, carpets, and fabrics. His unique wallpaper designs (fig. right) continue to be sold to this day. In Britain there followed a rehabilitation of crafts, and numerous workshops were set up. This was also the case in Germany, with the creation of the Deutsche Werkstätten (1898) in Dresden and the Deutscher Werkbund (1907, German Association of Craftsmen) in Munich. One could argue that it was out of these craft communities that modern design was born. Seeking to make up-to-date designs, they created the ideal

right—**WILLIAM MORRIS, STRAWBERRY THIEF WALLPAPER** | c. 1861

above——INTERIOR OF WILLIAM MORRIS'S RED HOUSE IN
BEXLEYHEATH

1883–1885—First skyscrapers in Chicago ·· 1896—First modern Olympic Games ··· **PIONEERS OF DESIGN** **14/15**

1887–1889—Eiffel Tower built in Paris ··

1891—Construction of Trans-Siberian Railway begins ······································

1886–1969 Ludwig Mies van der Rohe   **1887–1965 Le Corbusier**

environments for that new creature to emerge, the designer. Morris's floral designs are considered an inspiration for Art Nouveau, his ideas and ideals the basis of modernism.

It was also in Britain that the German architect Gottfried Semper wrote his revolutionary publications *Science, Industry and Art* (1852) and *Practical Aesthetics* (1860–1863). Despite the fact that he dealt only with classical Greek vessels, he nevertheless laid the theoretical foundation for modern design. He discussed the use and appearance of objects, stating that it is not merely useful for form to follow function, it is also simultaneously a guarantee of beauty. He also proclaimed a new art that he believed should accept industrialization and focus on pure forms. This constituted the theoretical foundation for functionalism, which some 60 years later would make its motto "Form follows function."

In Germany, Michael Thonet found a way to create a new style based on technical innovation with his bentwood furniture (see *Bentwood Furniture*). Thonet was able to combine the passion and skills of craftsmanship with the revolutionary spirit of industrialization, and he was among the first to produce furniture industrially. His acumen in managing his business contributed to his present-day status as the founder of modern furniture produc-

tion and as the most successful furniture manufacturer of the industrial age. The Thonet company set new standards in furniture-making: mass production made it possible to sell at affordable prices; the products were very light and yet strong; and transporting them unassembled lowered the cost. A worldwide sales network, participation in international exhibitions, large-scale advertising campaigns, and the printing of comprehensive catalogues helped to make Thonet famous throughout the world. The many and various furniture designs by Thonet have one thing in common: they combine artisanal design and industrial technology with elegance and high quality, and are to this day considered to be classics of furniture design.

Inspired by the British Arts and Crafts movement, the first pan-European style to create a new, uniform formal language developed at the turn of the twentieth century. This came to be known as *Jugendstil* in Germany, *Art Nouveau* in France, the *Modern Style* (and then *Art Nouveau*) in Britain, *Sezessionstil* in Austria, and *Modernismo* in Spain. In accordance with the notion of the *Gesamtkunstwerk*, the total work of art, it found expression in all fields of art, and pursued a connection between all disciplines, including architecture, the fine arts, and the crafts (and later design). An attempt was made to balance the perceived efficiency and tech-

16/17 *PIONEERS OF DESIGN* ··· **1900**—French Métro is opened·· **1919**—Bauhaus founded by Walter Gropius in Weimar···················
·· **1903**—Henry Ford establishes the Ford Motor Company in Detroit ·································
···**1914**—Beginning of World War I ···························

1902–1981 Marcel Breuer   **1907–1978 Charles Eames**

With its clear lines and its synthesis of all the arts to create a form appropriate to its time, Art Nouveau had a formative influence on the development of modernism.

nical nature of industrialization with the creation of original forms appropriate to their time that would appeal to the senses with beautiful decorations inspired by nature. The dynamically curved line was the basic element on which this artistic formal language was built. Like Arts and Crafts, Art Nouveau drew on the principles of artisanal production but showed a preference for modern materials such as iron, because its malleability made it versatile, and its strength meant it could be used to create highly intricate designs. Later developments in Art Nouveau, after 1900 in particular, are characterized by a reduced, more geometric design. The Scotsman Charles Rennie Mackintosh with his *Hill House Chair* (1904, fig. p. 8) and the Viennese Josef Hoffmann and his *Sitzmaschine* ("machine for sitting") (1905, fig. right) were particularly influential in this respect. With its clear lines and its synthesis of all the arts to create a form appropriate to its time, Art Nouveau had a formative influence on the development of modernism.

Opened in 1919, the Bauhaus school by contrast evangelically espoused what was called New Objectivity (Neue Sachlichkeit) (see *The Bauhaus*).

It considered itself to be a link between the arts, crafts, and industry, and went beyond a mere acceptance of industrialization: it considered industrial production to be an opportunity for a new, *modern* style. Classical modernism, as the Bauhaus style is most frequently known today, is therefore the first modern design style as defined here.

The situation was quite different on the other side of the Atlantic. Technical innovation was opposed by fewer traditions and met with less resistance in the United States than in "old Europe," making for a more accommodating and flexible response. Capitalism had created an enormous market for industrially produced utility objects, and products had to be made to look attractive in order to survive in this market. It was in the United States, therefore, that the profession of "industrial designer" first became viable.

right—**JOSEF HOFFMANN, SITZMASCHINE** | 1905

.... **1826**—First photography ....

.... **1830**—Opening of the Liverpool and Manchester Railway **18/19**

.... **1848**—Revolutions in numerous European countries ....

1796–1871 Michael Thonet

BENTWOOD FURNITURE: FLEXIBLE DESIGNS

The development of bentwood for the manufacture of furniture was one of the first great milestones of design as we understand it today. The oldest known method for bending wood into a particular shape had its origins in ship-building. Planks of wood were exposed to steam and then attached to curved beams while still hot. The wood could be bent only gently in this manner, however. A similar technique was used at the beginning of the nineteenth century in the production of wheels and barrels. The pieces of wood were boiled, then placed in a mold and left to cool and dry.

Michael Thonet, a carpenter from Boppard on the Rhine whose work was characterized by ambition, high standards, and perfectionism, further developed this method for furniture-making. Solid wood splinters on the outer curve when bent excessively, and so in 1830 he began to glue together multiple layers (laminates) of wood, before boiling and bending them. The Boppard laminated chair of 1836 (fig. p. 20) was his first great success. The external appearance did not yet truly reflect its rev-

olutionary inner construction, however. Its shape, like that of its predecessors, was enhanced by using pieces of carved wood. Those in the know, however, would have noticed its loop-shaped back, which points to its innovative production method. At a trade exhibition held at Johannisberg Castle in the Rheingau region, Thonet caught the attention of Count Metternich, who summoned the young entrepreneur to Vienna. Thanks to the patronage of Metternich, Thonet was able to work on his method in peace and quiet in the fashion-conscious and progressive metropolis. In 1842 he was granted a *privileg*, or patent, by the Austrian courts, allowing him to mold wood "using a chemical-mechanical process into any desired shape and form." As laminated wood could be bent in only one direction, and was very labor-intensive to produce, and as the chairs made in this way came unstuck when shipped to tropical climes, Thonet worked tirelessly to find a way to bend solid wood. One idea dating to 1856 consisted of attaching a thin, narrow steel splint to the outer side of the plank. This provided Thonet with his breakthrough. That same year he opened his first factory, in Korycany in the forested region of Moravia, where serial mass-production of his furniture began. Beech trunks were sawn into rectangular blocks of wood, cut into lengths, planed, and then smoothed and polished with sand-

left——MICHAEL THONET, CHAIR NO. 14 | 1859

paper. Next, the wood was bent over steam heated to 100 to 200 degrees Celsius, clamped into iron frames and allowed to dry. A high degree of stability could be achieved in this way, even with thin cross sections and tight curves. The bent elements could be joined using screws, and so the protracted gluing process could be dispensed with.

This production process made it possible for the first time to bend the wood two dimensionally, giving Thonet's designs an entirely new appearance. He developed a linear aesthetic that radiated lightness and elegance. The use of wood also imbued the pieces with a lively and natural air. This new style corresponded exactly with the desires of the aspirational, forward-looking middle classes of the nineteenth century. The groundbreaking elegance and lightness of Thonet's furniture thus found its way into private homes, and also became a common sight in cafés and restaurants thanks to its large production runs and low production costs. By World War II, 50 million copies of model *No. 14* (fig. p. 18), which became the archetype of the Viennese coffeehouse chair and is now considered to be the ultimate Thonet classic, had already been sold. It thus became the first "mass chair" and

made design history as the archetype of modern furniture design and the prototype of successful industrial design. Le Corbusier was a vocal Thonet enthusiast, and liked to use these bentwood chairs in his interior designs. He stated that "never before has anything been created that was more elegant or better in its conception, more exact in its execution, or fit for its use." The original goal of the model developed in 1859 was the creation of an affordable consumer chair that could be used in working-class homes, in offices, cafés, and bars. Thonet was in fact able to avoid raising the price of his "three-guilder chair" for more than 50 years. Consisting of just five parts, it did not take up much space and could be shipped across the world. Two aspects of Thonet's achievement are significant: he created the preconditions for serial mass-production, and his technical innovations changed

above——MICHAEL THONET, BOPPARD LAMINATED CHAIR | 1836
right——ALVAR AALTO, NO. 41 (PAIMIO) | 1931

1898–1976 Alvar Aalto   **1902–1971 Arne Jacobsen**   **1902–1981 Marcel Breuer**   **1904–1970 Egon Eiermann**   **1907–1978 Charles Eames**

the aesthetics of furniture; a new style grew out of this new technology and its production-related aesthetic. The *Viennese Chair*, as model *No. 14* is also known, is one of the few products developed in the nineteenth century to have survived the era in which it was created and continues to be valued as a classic.

The development of tubular furniture and the clean, straight lines of the Bauhaus style at the beginning of the twentieth century usurped bentwood furniture's preeminent position in furniture design. It gained significance once again in the 1930s, however. The development of new materials, such as modern glues made using synthetic materials, the evolution of new processing techniques, such as hydraulic presses, and the production of enormous sheets of veneer provided designers like Alvar Aalto, Marcel Breuer, and Charles and Ray Eames with a world of new possibilities for making furniture using wood. Aalto's first modern chair design, model *No. F35*, is a combination of a steel tube and plywood. For some, this looked like an awk-

22/23 BENTWOOD FURNITURE ··· **1914–1918**—World War I ·················· **1937**—Pablo Picasso, *Guernica* ························
1928—Alexander Fleming discovers penicillin ·········
1955—*The Family of Man* exhibition at MoMA in New York ··········

| 1912–1988 Ray Eames | 1914–2007 Hans J. Wegner | 1940–today Peter Karpf | 1949–today Beat Frank |

ward compromise employing both materials. Aalto, too, experimented for many years in order to create the ideal basis for furniture design. He considered wood to be the best material, satisfying not only the functional but also the psychological requirements of the user. He described his favorite construction material as a "form-inspiring, thoroughly human material." He soon presented his *Paimio* chairs, model *No. 41* (1931, fig. p. 21) and *No. 31* (1932, fig. p. 75). Groundbreaking in their use of plywood, they were cut and formed from a single sheet. With his *Paimio* chairs, Aalto managed to translate the rectilinear, modern Bauhaus aesthetic of tubular chairs into wood. With the removal of a few layers of the veneer, he was able to bend the rolled-up ends of the seat shell, which was thinner and more flexible as a result. For model *No. 31*, Aalto pushed the elasticity of the plywood so far that it became the first cantilever chair made of wood—a design that gave a friendlier face to modernism. Inspired by Aalto's plywood models, between 1935 and 1937 Marcel Breuer designed five models for Isokon that were essentially wood versions of his tubular-steel furniture.

The next breakthrough in wood bending was achieved by Charles and Ray Eames in the mid-1940s, in their kitchen. They were dissatisfied with the producers and manufacturers of plywood, who

were unwilling to experiment further with the material. Using bicycle parts, plaster components, and heated filaments, they managed to construct a machine that remains to the present day a model for bentwood production. It was named after the magic incantation "Alakazam," and created the first three-dimensionally bent plywood seat shell to be serially produced. Thin plywood veneers were layered with a synthetically based hot-melt adhesive between two casts. They were transformed into firm molded parts by pressing and heating them for between four and six hours. This method was also used in 1946 for the furniture in their *Plywood* series (fig. above), whose three-dimensional form allowed the pieces to be ergonomically adapted to the human body, and to be, like an egg, strong despite the thinness of the material. These experiments with three-dimensionally-formed plywood inspired countless other designers to conduct their

above——**Charles and Ray Eames, DCW Chair** | 1946
right——**Arne Jacobsen, model 3100 (Ant Chair)** | 1952
following pages——**Gebrüder Thonet, Chair No. 209, re-edition by Thonet GmbH**

26/27 BENTWOOD FURNITURE ··· **1965**—Beginning of Vietnam War·· **1995**—*Toy Story* is first movie produced entirely with computer animation·········

·· **1984**—Production of the first commercial cell phone ············

·· **2012**—Olympic Games in London ·············

own experiments. Egon Eierman constructed the *SE 42* in 1949, Arne Jacobsen made his *Ant* in 1952 (fig. p. 23), and Hans J. Wegner produced the elegantly vaulted *CH 07* in 1963.

But the improvements in synthetic materials with which the furniture industry increasingly experimented from the 1960s onwards led to a renewed loss of significance for bentwood. The bright colors, considerably lower costs, and the malleability of synthetics made them far better suited to the Pop aesthetic of the decade. Plywood was considered too bulky and unfashionable in the era of Minimalism that followed. Postmodernists preferred to cover up plywood instead of thinking creatively about its potential uses.

But serious furniture design using formed wood experienced a revival in the 1990s. After plastic kitsch (see *Pop Culture*) and colorful Memphis designs (see *Postmodernism*), wood was again put to use because of its natural beauty and simplicity. A new appreciation of the material also led to a renewed interest in the ways in which wood can be processed. Companies specializing in plywood worked in close cooperation with designers, and developed individual production processes for specific products. Innovations such as laser-based shaping machines, new computer programs, and

constantly improving adhesives and plywood now make it possible to exploit the possibilities inherent in the material further. The "bending" divan (fig. right) by Beat Frank from 2002 is a laser-cut design whose birch plywood is produced using a special glue. The wood is therefore very thin, yet simultaneously so strong that it can flex. It can be set up in three different ways, as a chaise longue, a divan, or a chair. The backrest of the *Sarno* office chair by Dirk Tegtmeyer for Züco is another good example, appearing to wrap effortlessly around a thin steel tube. Production for this piece is, however, very laborious, and the method is one of the manufacturer's well-kept secrets.

Nobody can predict what the future holds for formed wood. The XUS prototype (fig. above) by the Scandinavian designer Peter Karpf may provide an intimation, however: the laminated beech plywood is folded like a piece of fabric, forming a cantilever chair in which incredible lightness and elegance are coupled with an organic aesthetic.

above——PETER KARPF, XUS (PROTOTYPE)
right——BEAT FRANK, ÜBERDREHTE LIEGE | 2002

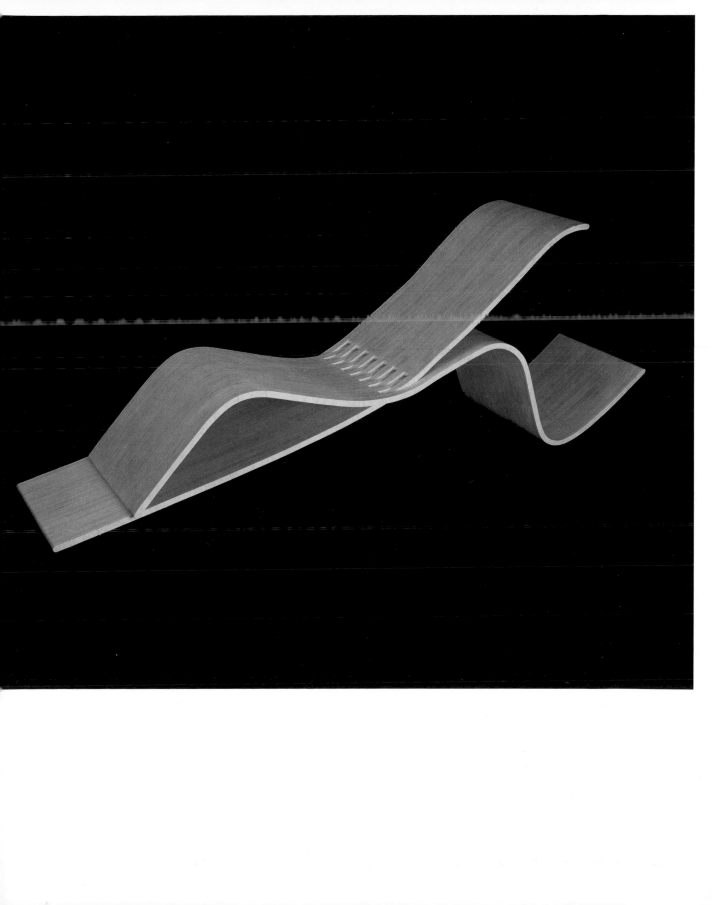

1837—Victoria becomes queen of the United Kingdom .... 1871—Charles Darwin publishes *The Descent of Men* ....
1851—John Ruskin, *The Stones of Venice* ....
1857–1859—First world economic crisis ....

28/29

1803–1879 Gottfried Semper　　　　　1834–1896 William Morris　　　　　1863–1957 Henry van de Velde

THE BAUHAUS: THE FIRST SCHOOL OF MODERN DESIGN

Opened in Weimar in 1919 under the direction of Walter Gropius (fig. right), the Bauhaus was the first successful institution whose specific aim was to train designer. The state-financed Bauhaus was thus the first school of modern design, and as such laid the foundation for what we now consider to be "design."

Although the Bauhaus was the first school of its kind, providing a comprehensive training for professionals in this field, it should be remembered that it was able to build on experiments and ideas that emerge during the nineteenth century. As discussed earlier (see *Pioneers of Design*), modern design is inextricably bound up with industrialization, and the first attempts to establish training courses for the new profession of designer were made in the homeland of industrialization: in Britain. This is where the Normal School of Design was founded in 1837, in London, with the aim of teaching elementary drawing and drawing for various industrial applications. It closed just two years later,

however, as there were not enough students. The great "crisis of style" that accompanied the London Great Exhibition of 1851 again raised the question throughout Europe of the need for a better education in industrial art. At this time, Gottfried Semper intended to establish a private art school in which he could bring together many of the principles that would in fact later underpin the Bauhaus when it opened 60 years later. Semper differentiated between the unthinking and the informed use of machines, wanted to unify architecture and the

left——Walter Gropius's director's office in the Bauhaus building in Weimar (reconstruction) | 1923
right——Walter Gropius | 1922

above——**Henry van de Velde, Bauhaus building in Weimar**
constructed 1904–1911
right—— **Edmund Collein** | **Students in the Gropius architecture**
department in Dessau | c. 1927 | photograph

1876—Invention of the telephone .... 1895—Discovery of X-rays ... THE BAUHAUS **30/31**

1886—Statue of Liberty erected in New York Harbor ....

1893—First issue of *The Studio* ....

1866–1944 Wassily Kandinsky   **1868–1940 Peter Behrens**   **1879–1940 Paul Klee**

visual and decorative arts, and considered workshop instruction to be the ideal way to teach. Although he published two influential books (*Science, Industry and Art* (1852) and *Practical Aesthetics* (1860–1863)), taught as a professor in the Department of Practical Art (later the Victoria and Albert Museum) in London, and worked according to the principles he adopted in his workshop, his desire for a school of his own was never realized. William Morris was another forerunner of the Bauhaus, pursuing a workshop philosophy and a revival of traditional crafts. He himself learned to weave in the Gobelin style in order to understand every aspect of the craft, which gave him a distinct advantage in the process of designing. He realized that one of the main causes of the low quality and bad taste that characterized the industrial arts of the nineteenth century was the fact that designs were made without a real understanding of materials or manufacturing. Morris and his followers were responsible for breaking down the boundaries between artists and craftsmen, who were at the time held in less esteem, so that artists were now to work on designs for everyday objects. Leading German architects Peter Behrens and Bruno Paul, as well as the Belgian Henry van de Velde, were greatly influenced by this British development. The decisive step, taken by the Germans but rejected outright by the British, was the acceptance of the machine. This was seen to be the only way in which a universal style, a style not exclusive to the rich, could be developed. It is to the great credit of the Deutscher Werkbund (German Association of Craftsmen) and of many German workshops that they responded to the requirements of industry and subordinated the standards of handcrafts to those of industrial art. This reforming tendency, represented by the Werkbund from 1900 to 1914, brought together architects and manufacturers to disseminate the new style together.

Together with these trailblazers, the Bauhaus was also inspired by the strong desire for change that developed following World War I—many felt a need to question traditional values in order create a new, better, future. The Bauhaus drew upon all these earlier developments, and pushed them much farther. Gropius set out very clearly what form this new type of training should take by formulating and putting into practice the aims and methods of the Bauhaus. He saw the Bauhaus as a link between art and the everyday, stating that it should "serve the contemporary developments in dwellings, from the humble home appliance to the completed residential building." The artist was in his view the epitome of the craftsman, and for this reason learning craft skills in a workshop setting was to form

the basis of their training. For Gropius, the Bauhaus workshops were "essentially laboratories in which prototypes of products suitable for mass production and typical of our time are carefully developed and constantly improved." Gropius wanted the Bauhaus to function as an intermediary between art, craft and industry by "training up a new, previously unknown type of worker, equally knowledgeable in technology and form, for industry and trade." In order to provide this training, Gropius gathered together an extraordinary, international body of instructors that included famous architects such as Hannes Meyer and Ludwig Mies van der Rohe, painters like Wassily Kandinsky, Johannes Itten, and Paul Klee, and craftsmen including Marcel

Breuer and Erich Dieckmann. This allowed him not only to pursue the ideal of the unification of the various disciplines to form a new Bauhaus style, but also to create a creative and avant-garde environment. Between 120 and 200 students were instructed at the Bauhaus each term. They all rotated through the six-month preparatory training program on which a distinctively holistic education was based. The aim was the dismantling of academ-

above—WALTER GROPIUS, BAUHAUS BUILDING IN DESSAU | 2008

1900—Boxer Rebellion in China ·· 1911—Wassily Kandinsky, *Concerning the Spiritual in Art*··· THE BAUHAUS **32/33**

1903—First powered flight by the Wright brothers··········

1907—*Werkbund* exhibition in Cologne·········

1883–1969 Walter Gropius   1886–1969 Ludwig Mies van der Rohe   1889–1954 Hannes Meyer

Walter Gropius saw the Bauhaus as a link between art and the everyday, stating that it should 'serve the contemporary developments in dwellings, from the humble home appliance to the completed residential building.'

ic perceptions, the recognition and encouragement of individual talent, and the acquisition of a basic design qualification. This was followed by a three-year traineeship in crafts, in which technical and artisanal skills were learned through practical experience in various workshops (glass, clay, stone, wood, metal, textile, and paint) and under the direction of master designers and master craftsmen. And finally there was architectural training, during which students made practical contributions to the various architectural projects undertaken by the Bauhaus. Gropius was interested not only in the training, but also in an all-round development of character that would transform students into skilled and responsible workers. The Bauhaus was therefore designed in a very democratic manner, the student council having a significant say. A program of theatre productions, lectures, discussions and concerts was designed to further strengthen the amicable relationship between students and teachers.

The Bauhaus era, which lasted only 14 years, can be divided into four phases. During the *foundation phase* (1919–1923), the Bauhaus was still heavily influenced by the art of Expressionism and by the artisanal ideals of the Arts and Crafts movement. A plethora of individually crafted pieces of furniture and household objects were produced

during this time. Gropius's director's office (fig. p. 28) was furnished exclusively with Bauhaus designs, and so also functioned as an exhibition space for the school's products. From 1922 Theo van Doesburg, who was a member of the Dutch De Stijl movement, gave guest lectures in which he criticised "individual," expressionist designs. This criticism, together with the first Bauhaus exhibition of 1923, led to a clearer sense of the Bauhaus's identity and a more precise statement of its aims. During what is known as the *consolidation phase* (1923–1928), the Bauhaus refocused on its original aim of supplying prototypes for industry. With its clear forms, the Bauhaus style now moved towards a sober functionalism. In 1925 budget cuts and rising criticism of the school in conservative Weimar caused the Bauhaus to relocate to Dessau. Thanks to the Social Democrat mayor Fritz Hesse, who was well disposed towards the Bauhaus, to the city's flourishing industry, and to the construction of a new school building designed by Gropius (fig. left), the Bauhaus flourished in Dessau. The most famous Bauhaus furniture designs were created during this period, when Marcel Breuer (who was himself a product of the Bauhaus) was in charge of the furniture workshop and introduced tubular furniture (see *Tubular Steel*). In the consolidation phase in particular, the Bauhaus was able to put

34/35 THE BAUHAUS ···················· **1915**—Kazimir Malevich, *Black Square* ····················· **1933**—Adolf Hitler comes to power

·······················**1919**—Founding of the Weimar Republic ····················

1925/1926—Walter Gropius, Bauhaus, Dessau····················

1902–1981 Marcel Breuer

One of the lasting achievements of the Bauhaus was the way in which it facilitated the development of a close relationship between art and industry at a time when there was a desire to produce objects that clearly reflected a modern way of life.

into practice ideas about contemporary forms of training and modern design. This was also necessary in order to remain financially independent, which is why Gropius always encouraged the manufacture of products that would sell well. Products designed by the Bauhaus, from lamps and chairs to wallpaper, furniture and crockery, and made widely available by German industry, proved that the "Bauhaus model" worked not only in theory but also in practice. One of the lasting achievements of the Bauhaus was the way in which it facilitated the development of a close relationship between art and industry at a time when there was a desire to produce objects that clearly reflected a modern way of life. New Objectivity (Neue Sachlichkeit), as the Bauhaus style was known, became the predominant style in Germany until the 1930s.

When Gropius left the Bauhaus in 1928 as a result of continuous hostility from conservative critics, the school underwent a number of changes. The *disintegration phase* (1928–1929) set in. Gropius's successor, Hannes Meyer, had strong socialist tendencies and

further developed low-cost industrial mass production, to the detriment of aesthetic considerations. Social housing and affordable furniture became the focus (fig. right). After just two years, Meyer was given notice because of his Marxist leanings. The fourth phase, the *final stage* (1930–1933), was shaped by Meyer's successor, Ludwig Mies van der Rohe. He transformed the Bauhaus into a conventional school of architecture. Less importance was attached to the workshops, students no longer gained practical experience, and the training period was shortened considerably. It was therefore hardly a surprise that the focus was shifted entirely from crafts to architecture. The Bauhaus, which had emphasised the practical, became a theoretical school of architecture. When it had to shut down on the orders of the National Socialists in 1932, Mies van der Rohe moved the Bauhaus once more. He chose the more liberal city of Berlin, where he wanted to continue to run it as a private institute. The hostility would not die down even there, however, and the Bauhaus closed its doors for good on 19 July 1933.

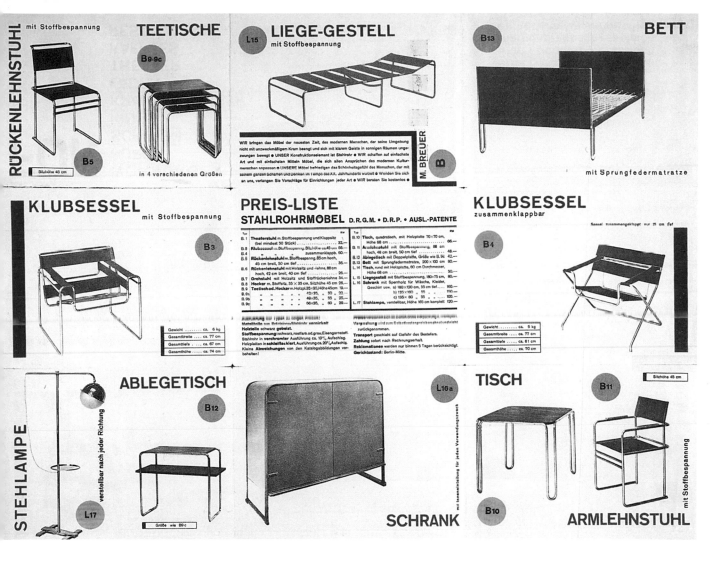

RÜCKENLEHNSTUHL mit Stoffbespannung

TEETISCHE B9-9c

in 4 verschiedenen Größen

LIEGE-GESTELL L15 mit Stoffbespannung

BETT B13

B5 Sitzhöhe 45 cm

WIR bringen das Möbel der neusten Zeit, des modernen Menschen, der seine Umgebung nicht mit unzweckmäßigem Kram beengt und sich mit klarem Geiste in sonnigen Räumen ungezwungen bewegt ● UNSER Konstruktionselement ist Stahlrohr ● WIR schaffen auf einfachste Art und mit einfachsten Mitteln Möbel, die sich allen Ansprüchen des modernen Kulturmenschen anpassen ● UNSERE Möbel befriedigen das Schönheitsgefühl des Menschen, der mit seinem ganzen Schaffen und Denken im Tempo des XX. Jahrhunderts wurzelt ● Wenden Sie sich an uns, verlangen Sie Vorschläge für Einrichtungen jeder Art ● WIR beraten Sie kostenlos

M. BREUER B

mit Sprungfedermatratze

KLUBSESSEL mit Stoffbespannung

PREIS-LISTE
STAHLROHRMÖBEL D.R.G.M. ● D.R.P. ● AUSL.-PATENTE

KLUBSESSEL zusammenklappbar

B3

Typ		RM
B.1	**Theaterstuhl** m. Stoffbespannung und Klappsitz (bei mindest 50 Stück)	32.—
B.3	**Klubsessel** m. Stoffbespannung, Sitzhöhe ca.45 cm	66.—
B.4	" " zusammenklapb.	60.—
B.5	**Rückenlehnstuhl** m. Stoffbespannung, 85 cm hoch, 45 cm breit, 50 cm tief	36.—
B.6	**Rückenlehnstuhl** mit Holzsitz und -lehne, 88 cm hoch, 42 cm breit, 40 cm tief	26.—
B.7	**Drehstuhl** mit Holzsitz und Stoffrückenlehne	34.—
B.8	**Hocker** m. Stoffsitz, 35 × 35 cm, Sitzhöhe 45 cm	26.—
B.9	**Teetisch od.Hocker** m.Holzpl.35×35,Höhe45cm	19.—
B.9a	" " 47×35, " 50	22.—
B.9b	" " 49×35, " 55	25.—
B.9c	" " 56×35, " 60	29.—

Typ		RM
B.10	**Tisch**, quadratisch, mit Holzplatte 70×70 cm, Höhe 68 cm	66.—
B.11	**Armlehnstuhl** mit Stoffbespannung, 86 cm hoch, 48 cm breit, 50 cm tief	48.—
B.12	**Ablegetisch** mit Doppelplatte, Größe wie B.9c	42.—
B.13	**Bett** mit Sprungfedermatratze, 200 × 100 cm	80.—
B.14	**Tisch**, rund mit Holzplatte, 60 cm Durchmesser, Höhe 68 cm	50.—
L.15	**Liegegestell** mit Stoffbespannung, 180×75 cm	60.—
L.16	**Schrank** mit Sperrholz für Wäsche, Kleider, Geschirr usw. a) 180×120 cm, 55 cm tief	160.—
	b) 135×190 " 55	150.—
	c) 135×80 " 55	100.—
L.17	**Stehlampe**, verstellbar, Höhe 165 cm komplett	120.—

Sessel zusammengeklappt nur 15 cm tief

B4

AUSFÜHRUNG NUR TYPEN ZU OBIGEN PREISEN!
Metallteile im Bektsinnsestahbrobr vernickelt.
Holzteile schwarz gebeizt.
Stoffbespannung: schwarz, rostfarb.od.grau, Eisengarnstoff.
Stahlrohr in verchromter Ausführung ca. 10%/ Aufschlag.
Holzplatten in schleiflackiert. Ausführung ca.20%/ Aufschlg.
Kleine Abweichungen von den Katalogabbildungen vorbehalten!

PREISE verstehen sich ab dort ohne Verpackung u. Transport.
Verpackung wird zum Selbstkostenpreis berechnet und nicht zurückgenommen.
Transport geschieht auf Gefahr des Bestellers.
Zahlung sofort nach Rechnungserhalt.
Reklamationen werden nur binnen 5 Tagen berücksichtigt.
Gerichtsstand: Berlin-Mitte.

Gewicht	ca. 6 kg
Gesamtbreite	ca. 77 cm
Gesamttiefe	ca. 67 cm
Gesamthöhe	ca. 74 cm

Gewicht	ca. 5 kg
Gesamtbreite	ca. 77 cm
Gesamttiefe	ca. 61 cm
Gesamthöhe	ca. 70 cm

STEHLAMPE verstellbar nach jeder Richtung

ABLEGETISCH B12

SCHRANK L16a mit Inneneinteilung für jeden Verwendungszweck

TISCH B11 Sitzhöhe 45 cm

ARMLEHNSTUHL mit Stoffbespannung

L17

Größe wie B9c

B10

1879—Albert Einstein is born .... 1897—Tate Gallery is founded in London ··· 36/37

1883–1885—First skyscrapers in Chicago ··

1887–1889—Eiffel Tower built in Paris ·······································

1878–1976 Eileen Gray 1886–1969 Ludwig Mies van der Rohe 1887–1965 Le Corbusier 1891–1982 René Herbst

TUBULAR STEEL: THE GLEAMING MACHINE AESTHETIC

Metal furniture existed even in antiquity: the Etruscans and the Romans, for example, used chairs made of bronze. From the mid-nineteenth century, when mechanical large-scale production began to replace hand-made craftsmanship as a consequence of the Industrial Revolution, there was a great expansion in the development of furniture made of metal. However, these chairs, stools, tables, and beds were made of cast or tubular metal and were not intended for domestic but for institutional use: in hospitals and sanatoriums, factories and prisons. Because of their enormous weight and unattractive appearance, they were not considered suitable for the home.

Welded-steel tubing was produced in Britain as early as 1825, but it was not until 1885 that the brothers Reinhard and Max Mannesmann successfully achieved a decisive technical development by inventing a "rotary piercing process" for the production of seamless pipes. In the "Mannesmann process," a heated rod of solid steel is turned between two convex rotating rollers and pulled over a mandrel to produce a seamless steel pipe. The result is a light steel tube that is durable and retains its shape; moreover, it can withstand high stress and is comparatively cheap. Mass production at the Mannesmann steel-tubing works in various locations throughout Europe meant that the new material was available everywhere. Initially, it was used only for industrial applications—for the frames of bicycles, for example.

And it was the handlebars of a bicycle—bent to shape, light and yet very strong—that inspired the designer and architect Marcel Breuer, a passionate cyclist, to design his first tubular-steel chair. Since 1920 Breuer had been working at the Bauhaus, where he first completed an apprenticeship as a carpenter and then, in 1925, became the head of the furniture workshop. At first he designed wooden furniture with simplified geometric shapes; the breakthrough came when he began to experiment with cold-bent steel tubing in 1925. With *B 3* (fig. left), the first chair made of tubular steel designed for domestic use (later known as the *Wassily Chair*) (1925–1926) (see *Design and Marketing*), he created the ancestor of all the items of tubular-steel furniture that have followed. In an age when the playfully ornamental designs of Art Nouveau dominated

left——MARCEL BREUER, B3 (WASSILY) CHAIR | 1925
following pages——LE CORBUSIER, PIERRE JEANNERET, CHARLOTTE PERRIAND, CHAISE LONGUE LC4 | 1927/1928

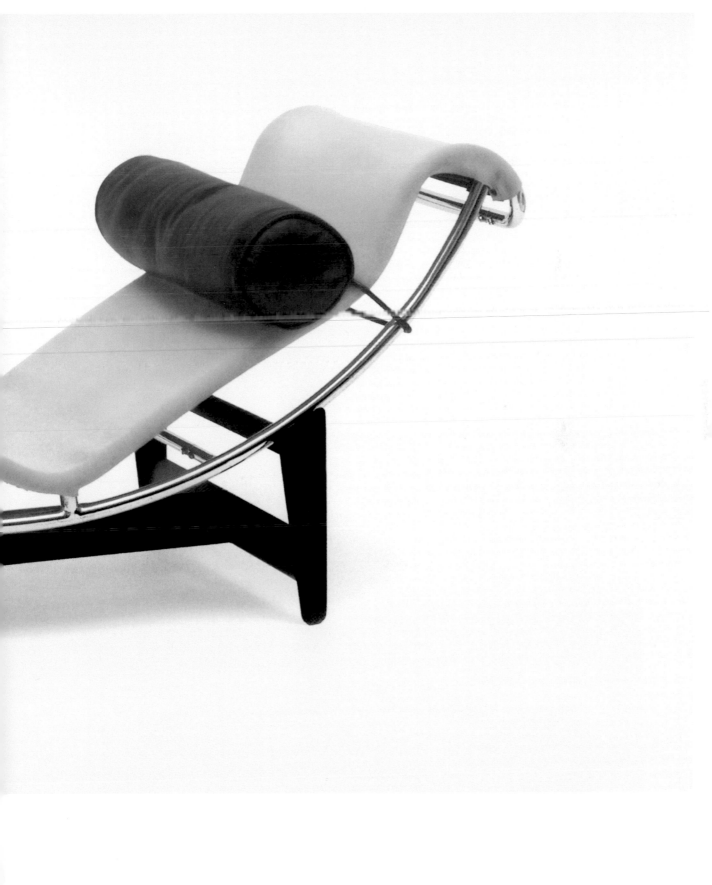

............**1901**—Queen Victoria dies ....**1907**—Pablo Picasso, *Les Demoiselles d'Avignon*... **TUBULAR STEEL** 40/41

....**1903**—Henry Ford establishes the Ford Motor Company in Detroit ....

....**1905**—German Expressionist group Die Brücke is founded in Dresden...

The clear, unfussy shape of tubular-steel furniture and its light and airy appearance seemed to embody the dawn of the modern age.

the living room, the cool tube of chrome-plated steel and the seat made of wire-mesh webbing certainly looked revolutionary.

Cold-bent steel tubing proved to be precisely the material with which the Bauhaus designers were able to realize both their aesthetic goals and their interest in industrial manufacturing processes and materials. The clear, unfussy shape of tubular-steel furniture, its transparency and functionality, and its light and airy appearance reflected a new, sober style; the use of steel tubing seemed to embody the dawn of the modern age. The chrome- or nickel-plating of the precision steel tubing gave the furniture its classic, chilly "machine aesthetic." Breuer wrote of his invention several years later: "A chair frame made of high-quality tubular steel (a very flexible material), with the addition of tightly stretched material where necessary, results in a light seating element with its own inherent suspension. It has the comfort of an upholstered seat but the difference is that it is considerably lighter, more convenient and hygienic, in other words much more practical to use."

Closely linked with the development of tubular-steel furniture is the cantilever chair without back legs, another design innovation of the twentieth century. Here a single length of metal tubing is used to form the legs, seat, and backrest of the chair (see *The Cantilever Chair*). Like Breuer, the Dutch architect Mart Stam had experimented with tubular steel, creating the original version of the cantilever chair in 1926. However, he strengthened the tighter curves of the gas piping he was using, so that the chair could not bounce, with the result that it was not as elegant as later models.

Ludwig Mies van der Rohe and Le Corbusier were also fascinated by the possibilities of the material, so that they too designed items of furniture using steel tubing. For the dining room of the Villa Tugendhat in Brno, Mies van der Rohe designed a variation on the cantilever chair made of tubular steel (*MR 20*); for his famous *Barcelona* armchair (*MR 90*), which he designed for the German pavilion at the World Fair in Barcelona in 1929, however, he used elegant steel bands instead of the rather functional tubing. At the suggestion of the French designer Charlotte Perriand, Le Corbusier also turned his attention to tubular-steel furniture in order to realize his ideal of the "machine for living." He combined organic forms that adapted to the body's shape with an austere metal structure. Thus

left——Eileen Gray, E 1027 occasional table | 1927

1911—Ernest Rutherford develops his model of the atom ·· **1925**—F. Scott Fitzgerald, *The Great Gatsby* ·····
··· **1914**—Marcel Duchamp's first readymade, *Bottle Rack* ··
·· **1919**—Bauhaus founded by Walter Gropius in Weimar ···

1920–1965 Hans Gugelot   **1924–2012 Fritz Haller**

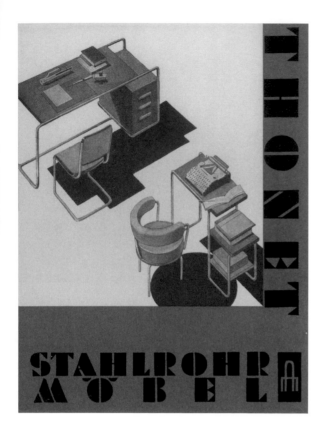

in his *Grand Confort* armchair (1927/1928), soft cushions are set into a bent frame of chrome-plated steel tubing. There is one chair in a narrow version, ideal for the male posture, and another broader version for the female sitting position, with the legs crossed to one side. Le Corbusier's *Chaise Longue LC4* (1927/1928, fig. pp. 38/39) also reflects an ergonomic adaptation to the human body. The actual lounger lies on an H-shaped metal frame with upholstery of fur or leather, and the curving shape imitates the silhouette of a resting body—in the words of its designer, a "true machine for resting." After the relatively sparse covering of the early models, before long luxuriously upholstered items of furniture made of tubular steel were also being created. The Irish designer Eileen Gray achieved new heights with the massive upholstery of her *Bibendum* armchair (1929). In contrast to the sober Bauhaus designs, this armchair radiates an element of irony—the three round cushions make humorous reference to the Michelin tire mascot Bibendum. Even more famous is her occasional table *E 1027* (1927, fig. p. 40), a small item of furniture made of tubular steel and plate glass for her villa on the Côte d'Azur, which in those days was considered the most elegant modern interior in France. The height of the table can be adjusted and with its semicircular foot it can also be pushed under a bed. The handle enables it to be moved around easily. Also of note is the *Sandow* chair (1928). Inspired by bodybuilding equipment, the French designer René Herbst stretched rubber cords across a frame of nickel-plated steel tubing to form a seat. Innovative tubular-steel furniture was presented to a wide-ranging public in 1927 at the Werkbund exhibition *Die Wohnung* (The Home), which was held on the Weissenhof estate in Stuttgart. The exhibition *Der Stuhl* (The Chair), held in Stuttgart the following year, also caused a stir. Tubular-steel furniture attracted international attention when,

......1929—The Museum of Modern Art opens in New York...1942—Edward Hopper, *Nighthawks*... TUBULAR STEEL

..............1931—Completion of the Empire State Building by William van Alen...................................

1933—Adolf Hitler comes to power....................................

42 /43

1928–today Luigi Colani   1932–today Dieter Rams   1935–today Norman Foster   1940–today Giancarlo Piretti

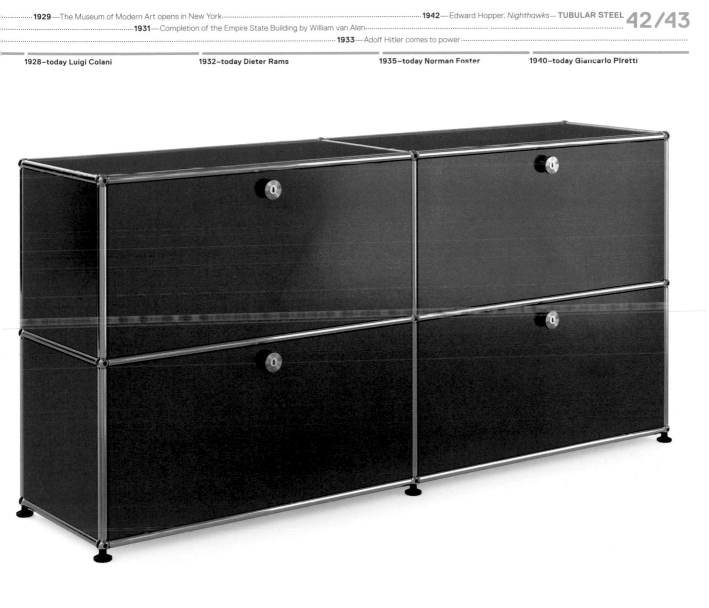

left——**FLYER FOR TUBULAR-STEEL FURNITURE BY THONET** | 1930s
above——**PAUL SCHÄRER, FRITZ HALLER, USM HALLER SIDEBOARD** | 1963

for example, it was shown at the World Fair of 1933 in Chicago. The use of steel was praised as being in step with the times. So it was only "natural, therefore that the modern spirit should express itself in striking, radically different kinds of furniture, and that furniture should be of steel, for this is the age of steel, and steel sounds the keynote of practica-bility, energy, and strength which dominates our modern life."

As early as the late 1920s, a number of firms began to specialize in the manufacture of modern tubular-steel furniture, including Standard-Möbel, Berliner Metallgewerbe Joseph Müller, Wohnbedarf Zürich, and Thonet. The last-named furniture maker, who had established a worldwide reputation with the manufacture of bentwood furniture, developed a second important area of activity with the tubular-steel furniture of classical modernism. By the early 1940s Thonet had at its disposal the biggest tubular-steel furniture program in Europe; to this day the company produces classics

1945—End of World War II ···   **1961**—Construction of the Berlin Wall·····················

1955—First *documenta* exhibition in Kassel, Germany ·······························

1959—First happening by Allan Kaprow ···················

1949–today Philippe Starck   **1960–today Karim Rashid**

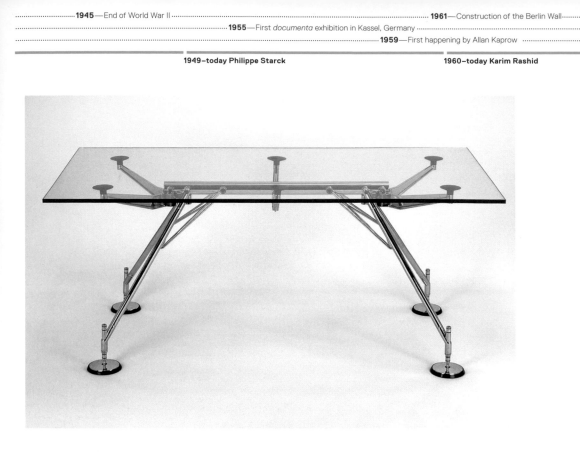

by Breuer, Stam, Mies van der Rohe, and others, in some cases unchanged and in others as special editions.

The tremendous enthusiasm for tubular-steel furniture faded considerably during the 1940s, however, not least because of the wide availability of the new material plastic (see *Plastic*). Steel tubing was increasingly sidelined into the sphere of office furniture. Here too, however, notable designs were produced. Pioneering to this day is the office furnishing system by the Swiss firm USM (fig. p. 43), designed in 1963 by engineer Paul Schärer in partnership with architect Fritz Haller. The key element of this modular furniture system is a chrome-plated aluminum ball whose holes are used to support a tubular-steel grid-frame into which metal surfaces can be slotted. This permits the creation of an office system that can be extended and altered as required.

It was at this time that the Bauhaus classics were rediscovered, and their popularity has continued unabated ever since. One example is Marcel Breuer's *S 285* desk (fig. right) from 1935, which has lost nothing of its modernity. The wooden elements—tabletop and drawers—are fitted into the tubular-steel frame shaped in an endless loop like an "N" in such a way that they appear to hover. The overall effect is one of great lightness and harmony. In 1987 Sir Norman Foster designed the *Nomos* writing desk series (fig. above) for the Italian office furnishing company Tecno: a deliberately technical, sober yet luxurious construction of steel, aluminum, and glass. Splayed legs and aluminum supports emerge from a tubular-steel frame on which rests a sheet of glass. The elegant steel structure has various additional elements and surfaces that make it very adaptable, so that a wide range of table configurations are possible. Tubular-steel furniture has also enjoyed a renaissance since the 1960s. One notable example is Giancarlo Piretti's *Plia* folding chair (1969), which combines a shiny tubular-steel frame with a seat and backrest of transparent plastic, thereby appealing by virtue of its visual lightness. *CH*

·············**1962**—Andy Warhols *Campbell's Soup Cans* ·· **1969**—Neil Armstrong is the first man on the moon ···· **TUBULAR STEEL** 44/45

1965–1975—Vietnam War ···

1963–today Marc Newson

left——**Norman Foster, Nomos writing desk** | 1987
above——**Marcel Breuer, S 285 desk** | 1935

1866–1944 Wassily Kandinsky　　1902–1981 Marcel Breuer　　1907–1978 Charles Eames

DESIGN AND MARKETING: HOW DESIGN CLASSICS ARE CREATED

Marcel Breuer's *B3* chair (1925, fig. left) represents a milestone in design. It was not only the first chair to be made from tubular steel, and therefore an ancestor of all later tubular-steel furniture (see *Tubular Steel*); with this chair Breuer also succeeded for the first time in transferring the new ideals of the Bauhaus (lightness, functionality, and the machine aesthetic) to furniture design. Moreover, it was this chair whose particular construction sparked off a re-thinking of the basic structure of chairs, eventually leading to the creation of the chair without back legs (see *The Cantilever Chair*), thereby paving the way for a completely new type of furniture design.

It is not surprising that this chair was awarded yet another place of honor: the *B3* was, literally, the first design classic. The Italian furniture manufacturer and design expert Dino Gavina, an astute businessman, traveled to New York in 1962 and convinced Marcel Breuer that he should permit him to revive a new edition of his tubular-steel chair and put it into series production. For the new edition of the *B3*, Gavina used the expression "design classic" for the first time, creating a catchy expression that forms an essential part of our modern vocabulary. The expression "design classic" is neither protected nor indeed clearly defined to this day, which has led to a certain inflationary use. Through the new category "classic," the chair acquired a status that led to an enormous increase in value—the expression "design classic" had become a marketing instrument.

Bauhaus fan Gavina was convinced that rational and functional design would sell even better with the addition of a little emotion in the crisis-ridden postwar years. In contrast to the Bauhaus, which consciously refrained from using associative or poetic product names, Gavina searched for a new name for the *B3*. An anecdote maintained that Breuer had given the first example of his revolutionary chair to his Bauhaus colleague Wassily Kandinsky for him to use in his living room. Gavina used this tale as a pretext for naming the chair after the abstract artist. And so the chair was presented to the public in a new way: the *B3* was humanized and given a mystique, and this led to a renewed enthusiasm for the furniture of the modern age. Proof of the success of this promotional measure is shown by the fact that the original name of the furniture item was suppressed, so that today the chair is virtually always known by its marketing name, as the *Wassily Chair*. The Italian's skill initiat-

left——MARCEL BREUER, B3 (WASSILY) CHAIR | 1925

1921—Arnold Schoenberg invents twelve-tone music ········· **late 1930s**—Global economic crisis··· **DESIGN AND MARKETING** 48/49

1925—Invention of television ·········

1928—Andy Warhol is born ·········

1917–2007 Ettore Sottsass   1926–1998 Verner Panton   1928–today Luigi Colani

ed a revival of Bauhaus furniture, the so-called "second age of modernism." It was not least as a result of this skillful marketing strategy that the *Wassily Chair* became the most famous and most-copied item of design furniture. Gavina's marketing strategy of extracting a single design product out of the endless mass of everyday objects in this way was soon adopted by many others and transformed the design world.

The use of emotion that Gavina had employed for the first time reached its zenith in the 1980s. Once again the impetus came from Italy. The Memphis group expressly rebelled against rational functionalism: they wanted to arouse emotions in a targeted way with their designs (see *Postmodernism*). In addition to the playful, colorful, ornate design, the name of a product was now particularly important—as it had been for Gavina. The name became part of the designs and told a story from the outset. This approach, which designers now also adopted, provided manufacturers with new sales and marketing strategies. Big firms like Alessi, Vitra, and

FSB recognized the strategy's potential and started producing experimental editions. Alberto Alessi in particular, who had become chairman of Alessi in 1970, expanded this form of cooperation, producing limited and signed series by internationally famous designers and architects. It was his aim to introduce design into everyday life through the emotional relationship between people and objects, and he was even prepared to design trivial objects like fly swatters and lavatory brushes. This led to what came to be known as "author designs," in which the designer, rather like the author of a book, was actually named. This principle remains very popular with major manufacturers to this day, because in this way the focus can be directed towards the designer and the product, enabling to be marketed more effectively. Designers are in a special position here: since they are freelance entrepreneurs and not employees of the manufacturer, they can develop independently to a large extent and can create a distinctive signature that is then visible in every product they design. Many of today's design classics were created with the help of author designs.

The *Graves Family* (fig. left) by Michael Graves and Alessandro Mendini's *Anna G.* corkscrew for Alessi (fig. above) ensured that design acquired a distinctive face—quite literally. The old slogan "Form follows function" became "Family follows fiction": the

left——MICHAEL GRAVES, 9093 KETTLE | 1985
above——ALESSANDRO MENDINI, ANNA G. CORKSCREWS | 1994

.... **1936–1939**—Spanish Civil War.. **1942**—Peggy Guggenheim opens the gallery Art of this Century in New York..

.... **1939**—Germany invades Poland; World War II commences..

.... **1940**—McDonalds is founded ....

1931–today Alessandro Mendini   **1934–today Michael Graves**

Philippe Starck succeeded in designing a kitchen appliance like a miniature sculpture: people bought the Juicy Salif lemon squeezer because it looked stylish, not because it was practical.

function and the object were personified, and even a product series boldly turned into a family. The French architect and designer Philippe Starck in particular understood how to give each of his products a very personal accent. He was especially fond of playing with humorous, sometimes ironic, product names. Among his best-known and most successful designs are the *Hot Berta* kettle (1990), the *Joe Cactus* ashtray (1990) (which looks like a cactus in a pot), the *Jim Nature* television set (1994) (100 percent recyclable), and the *Louis Ghost* chair (2002) (a transparent-plastic Renaissance-style shape). In combination with his masterly self-promotion, a sort of personality cult arose around Starck. The star designer—and with him another, infinitely more lucrative, marketing opportunity—was born. In 1990, with the *Juicy Salif* lemon squeezer (fig. right), Philippe Starck even eventually succeeded in designing a kitchen appliance like a miniature sculpture. People bought it because it looked stylish and came with a well-known name, not because it was practical. In fact, the lemon squeezer was anything but practical: it dripped and wobbled, and the material was attacked by the acid in the lemon juice—and yet it was still a huge sales success, because the feelings it called forth sparked off the "must-have" response. A relatively recent development is the manufacture of miniature collections. Firms like Vitra and Alessi

in particular are pioneers in this new marketing idea for design classics. The Vitra Design Museum had the idea of producing a miniatures collection, which to date comprises almost 80 models from international design history since 1850. The miniatures are produced by hand on a scale of 1:6. With its almost 30 miniature copies of everyday objects, Alessi wants to give collectors in particular the possibility of "completing their private collection with real objects in a manner that is economical as regards both space and money." Vitra, however, goes one step further. In line with the idea of a museum, the little chairs are also intended for use as study objects in training colleges and universities. Other manufacturers like Rosenthal and Iittala have followed suit and now produce miniature versions of great designs. The Danish company aptly named 1:6 Design specializes in this field and produces *only* miniature furniture. Although the objects lose their function through being miniaturized, they nonetheless gain in significance. They are transformed into icons and become symbols of status and style, thereby emphasizing the importance of design in modern society.

right—**PHILIPPE STARCK, JUICY SALIF LEMON SQUEEZER** | 1990

.... **1946**—First computer .... **1969**—Woodstock Festival ··· **DESIGN AND MARKETING** **50/51**
.... **1955**—Beginning of Pop Art ....
.... **1959**—First Barbie doll ....

1949–today Philippe Starck   **1951–today Ron Arad**   **1967–today Jonathan Ive**

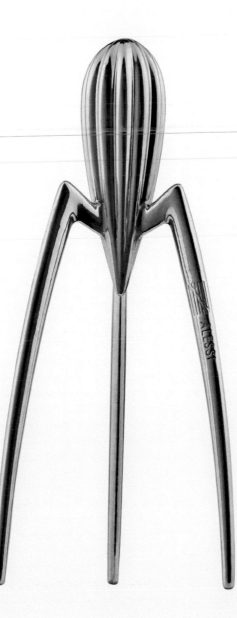

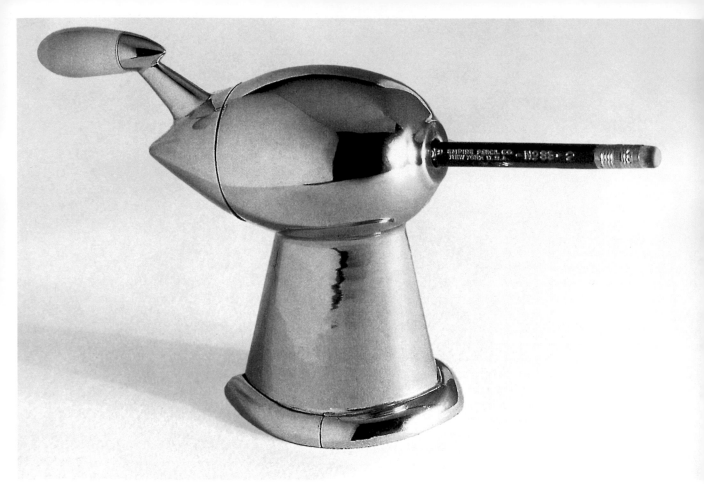

······················1883—First motor vehicle with internal combustion engine ··· 1892—First *VOGUE* issue in the U.S.····

·· 1883–1885—First skyscrapers in Chicago··

··· 1884—Mark Twain publishes *The Adventures of Huckleberry Finn* ································

52/53

1883–1960 Walter Dorwin Teague   **1893–1958 Norman Bel Geddes**   **1893–1986 Raymond Loewy**

STREAMLINE DESIGN: THE AESTHETICS OF SPEED

In October 1949, a cover of *Time Magazine* was devoted to French-born designer Raymond Loewy, noting that "he streamlines the sales curve." This was the first time that an industrial designer had attracted so much media attention. Loewy had provided an unparalleled impetus to the flagging US economy with his Streamline designs, which he made popular using clever marketing strategies. He was one of the first to recognize that the success of a product depends not only on its quality and functionality, but also on its design and "image." As the central figure of American industrial design, he was thus second to none in his influence on the appearance of everyday life, of the "American Way of Life," not least because the list of his clients reads like a Who's Who of American corporate giants: Lucky Strike, Coca-Cola, Greyhound, Shell, NASA, and Studebaker, to name but a few. Henry Dreyfuss, Norman Bel Geddes, Harold van Doren, Donald Deskey, and Walter Dorwin Teague are among the most important of Raymond Loewy's fellow representatives of Streamline (sometimes know as Streamform) design.

The American economy, which had stagnated following the collapse of the stock markets in 1929, found itself confronted by very strong competition in the years that followed. For the first time in history, design became the prime selling point, in particular where technical equipment was concerned. The demand for beautiful, newly designed objects grew. At the same time, technical innovations and constantly faster means of transportation (such as airplanes, automobiles, buses, and railroad locomotives) cried out for new designs. Streamlined shape as a technical prerequisite for the maximization of speed thus became the new face of the modern, of progress. Zeitgeist, function, and form became a symbolic unit through Streamline design.

The term "streamlining" was coined to describe scientific studies aiming to reduce air resistance, which became important as vehicles became progressively faster, with a variety of forms undergoing tests to determine their aerodynamic properties. Streamlines are those lines that are formed along bodies in wind tunnels. As is often the case, nature served as inspiration: throughout the process of evolution, fish and birds have developed to reduce as much as possible their resistance in water and air in order to make the best possible use of the energy they expend on movement. The pointed water-drop shape is particularly aerodynamic, so

left—**RAYMOND LOEWY, PENCIL SHARPENER** | 1933

54/55 STREAMLINE DESIGN ⋯**1893**—Edvard Munch, *The Scream*⋯⋯⋯⋯⋯⋯⋯⋯⋯⋯⋯⋯⋯⋯⋯⋯⋯ **1902**—Alfred Stieglitz's magazine *Camera Work* is founded
1895—Discovery of X-rays⋯⋯⋯⋯⋯⋯⋯⋯⋯⋯⋯
1901—Theodore Roosevelt sworn in as president of the U.S.⋯⋯⋯⋯⋯⋯⋯

1894–1989 Donald Deskey   1895–1957 Harold van Doren   1899–1973 Robert Heller

flowing, rounded forms that taper off at the back are characteristic of streamlined, and Streamline, design. Despite the fact that this type of design was based on scientific experiments, technology was not able to keep pace, and Streamline design was often nothing more than a symbolic illusion. The Pennsylvania Railroad's Streamline locomotive *S 1*, the Greyhound bus, and the Studebaker *Starliner* (all designs by Raymond Loewy), in addition to countless other automobile designs, achieved great fame. With their new, polished, futuristic image, they competed with airplanes. The Amer-

ican Hudson and the British Mallard locomotives have retained to this day their world records for steam locomotives, the latter reaching speeds of up to 125.88 mph (202.58 km/h) in 1938, and are the foundation upon which today's high-speed trains are built. The most famous automobiles of this time include the Tatra *77* (1934), the Chrysler *Airflow* (1934), the Studebaker *Commander* (fig. right), the Volkswagen *Beetle* (1938), and the Studebaker *Avanti* (1962). They are now in demand as classics. Even less-well-known prototypes with more extreme forms, such as the A.L.F.A. *40-60 HP* (1914)

left——STREAMLINE LOCOMOTIVE BY ROBERT STEPHENSON &
HAWTHORNS | 1940
above——STUDEBAKER COMMANDER STATE CONVERTIBLE | 1951

1903—Henry Ford establishes the Ford Motor Company in Detroit ·············· 1927— Charles Lindbergh flies nonstop from New York to Paris ············

1906—San Francisco earthquake ·············

1913—Armory Show in New York shows the European avant-garde ·············

1904–1972 Henry Dreyfuss   1908–1994 Max Bill   1920–1965 Hans Gugelot

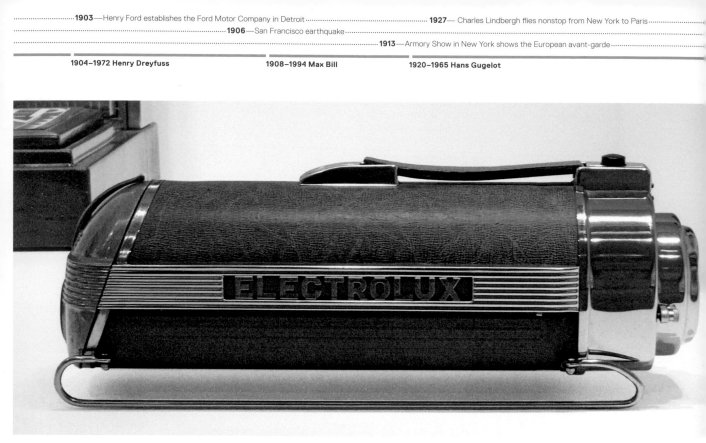

and the Ley *T6* (1922), are remarkable studies, and provided important inspiration for the construction of modern automobiles.

Purpose-designed streamlined form soon became a symbol of movement, speed, and therefore of progress and change. American designers liked to remark that "streamlining is cleanlining," as they attempted in their designs to "clean" objects of any bothersome elements, to make them melt into an evenness and uniformity. Machines were thus hidden under smoothed metal coverings, and details such as knobs and handles were masked or rounded. This effect was underlined by the use of polished chrome and steel, the shiny surfaces making the design look even more dynamic. This can also

be regarded as a symbol of mass production. The movement to increase hygiene and health at this time was almost literally reflected in the sparkling, smooth surfaces of the new objects.

Inspired by the aerodynamic experiments on means of transport, Streamline design was increasingly applied to technically sophisticated everyday objects. This resulted in vacuum cleaners (*Model 30* by Lurelle Van Arsdale Guild for Electrolux,

above—LURELLE VAN ARSDALE GUILD, MODEL 30 VACUUM CLEANER 1937

1929—Stock market crash heralds global economic crisis··· 1939–1945—World War II···STREAMLINE DESIGN 56/57
···1930—Grant Wood, *American Gothic*···
··1936—Charlie Chaplin, *Modern Times*··

1926–1998 Verner Panton   1932–today Dieter Rams

The purpose-designed streamlined form soon became a symbol of movement, speed, and therefore of progress and change.

1937, fig. left), refrigerators (*Coldspot* by Raymond Loewy, 1937), hairdryers (*Eskimo* hairdryer), table fans (*Airflow* by Robert Heller, 1937), desk lamps (*Model 114 "Executive"* by Walter Dowin Teague for Polaroid, 1939), and pressing irons (by Henry Dreyfuss for General Electric, 1948). And so dynamic forms and modern designs found their way into households as well and came to represent not only progress and mechanization, but also the new confidence—and buying power—of the housewife.

The terms "re-design" and "styling" are intimately linked to this development. They describe the superficial reworking of existing products to make them visually more appealing and so increase sales. Company logos, as well as everyday objects, underwent the process of renewal. During the course of his career, Raymond Loewy gave a new appearance to the Greyhound logo (a running greyhound) (1933), the Lucky Strike pack (1940, fig. p. 58), the Coca-Cola bottle (1954), and the Shell Company "shell" (1967).

In 1933 Loewy developed a prototype of Streamline design in the form of a pencil sharpener (fig. p. 52). This simple object combines various characteristics of the era, and of Loewy himself. It has the water-drop form typical of Streamline design, and escapes its inherent banality through its extraordinary appearance. This "elevation of status"

was always part of Loewy's design philosophy, attempting to imbue every object with a certain glamour. It made no difference to him whether he was designing a shaver or an automobile, which is why he was given the catchphrase "lipstick to locomotive." Even a simple object like a pencil sharpener becomes a futuristic sculpture that looks as though it is about to take off. This also reveals the obsession of the time: everything had to be molded into a dynamically flowing, new, modern form, even a pencil sharpener, which surely has no need to be streamlined in order to perform its function.

And this is precisely the criticism leveled at Streamline design. Europeans in particular were not impressed by what they regarded the superficial over-designing of objects. Max Bill, a member of the celebrated Hochschule für Gestaltung Ulm (Ulm School of Design) and a proponent of "good form," was their standard bearer. Despite the fact that during the postwar years both styles stood in opposition to reactionary bourgeois values and advocated a new, modern ideal, they had very different design philosophies. The Europeans described Streamlining as "false modernism" and criticized it for merely decorating and masking, rather than really creating something new. In fact, few wind-tunnel experiments were carried out,

..........................**1949**—Founding of the North Atlantic Treaty Organization···**1959**—Completion of the Solomon R. Guggenheim Museum in New York

······························**1950**–**1953**—Korean War ··

··········· **1955**–**1968**—Civil rights movement in the U.S.························

1949–today Philippe Starck   **1951–today Ron Arad**   **1959–today Massimo Iosa Ghini**

and the streamlined form of many everyday objects was often purely superficial and devoid of meaning. Moreover, truly streamlined vehicles such as the *Tropfenwagen* ("Drop Car") designed by Edmund Rumpler (1921) and the Chrysler *Airflow* (1934) failed on the market. Loewy was always aware of this criticism. His designs were about the sensory perception experienced when looking at and touching objects: "The forms awaken all sorts of unconscious associations—the simpler the form, the more pleasant the feeling elicited by it." Loewy's work continues to look modern today because he used his sense of aesthetics to give objects the magic aura they had lost.

In the late 1980s Streamline form was used as a stylistic device by proponents of New Design. Massimo Iosa Ghini and Marc Newson, for example, designed furniture that drew heavily on its curved lines and shiny, curved chrome. Newson's 1986 *Lockheed* lounge chair (fig. right) made from aluminum is an impressive example of the revival of the Streamline design of the 1930s.

1961—Yuri Gagarin is the first man in space···········1969 —Neil Armstrong is the first man on the moon··· STREAMLINE DESIGN 58/59

1963—Martin Luther King's "I have a dream" speech

1966–1973—Construction of the World Trade Center in New York

1963–today Marc Newson   1967–today Jonathan Ive

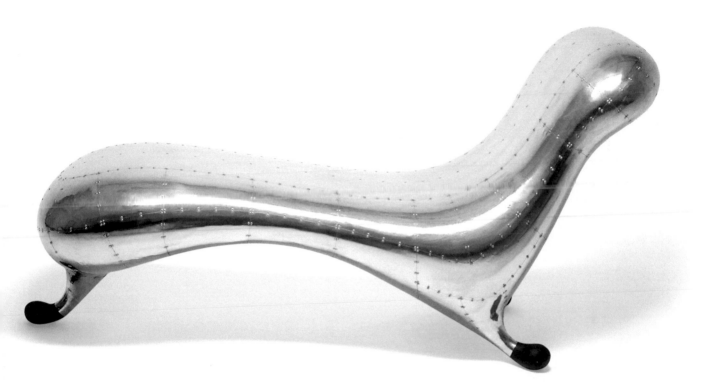

left——RAYMOND LOEWY, LUCKY STRIKE PACK | 1940
above——MARC NEWSON, LOCKHEED LOUNGE CHAIR | 1986

1879—Thomas Alva Edison invents carbon-filament light bulbs .... 1911—German artist group Der Blaue Reiter is founded in Munich···
1897—Artist movement Vienna Secession is founded in Vienna ···
1903—Kraft Foods is founded ·····························

60/61

1868–1940 Peter Behrens   1900–1990 Wilhelm Wagenfeld   1910–1977 Eliot Noyes

CORPORATE DESIGN— CORPORATE IDENTITY

In a world dominated by competition, strong, easily recognizable brands play an important role. They provide orientation for the purchaser, encourage brand loyalty, and enable a company to set itself apart from its rivals. It hardly seems possible that at the beginning of the twentieth century mass-produced objects seldom achieved harmony of form and function. Aesthetic considerations were virtually ignored in the case of industrially produced items, and companies paid little if any attention to creating a uniform corporate image. This was all changed by Peter Behrens, who was not only the father of German industrial design, but also the inventor of corporate identity.

AEG (Allgemeine Elektricitäts-Gesellschaft) was founded in 1887 in Berlin. After its founder Emil Rathenau had acquired the patents of the American inventor Thomas Edison for light bulbs in 1883, within the space of a few years the firm had expanded to become a worldwide concern. Less than two decades later AEG's innovative and

wide-ranging products extended from kettles (fig. above), vacuum cleaners, and electric stoves to rail and road vehicles, as well industrial installations and marine equipment. On a technical level, AEG's products were groundbreaking; but little was done to demonstrate this fact through their visual appearance, or through the way the company itself was presented. Products that were ultra-modern from a technical point of view were designed in a

left——DEVELOPMENT OF THE AEG LOGO FROM 1896 TO TODAY
right——PETER BEHRENS, TEA-KETTLE FOR AEG | c. 1913

1914—*Werkbund* exhibition in Cologne ·· 1928—Walt Disney creates Mickey Mouse··· CORPORATE DESIGN 62/63

1917—U.S. entry into World War I··

1921—Albert Einstein awarded the Nobel Prize for Physics ······························

1914–1996 Paul Rand   1917–2007 Ettore Sottsass   1920–1965 Hans Gugelot   1922–1991 Otl Aicher

Dieter Rams's products—from record players and electric razors to kettles and other kitchen appliances, as well as hair dryers and calculators—set design standards for clarity and minimalist design.

non-uniform and often old-fashioned way and were accompanied by a curving company emblem in Art Nouveau letters (fig. p. 60).

In 1906 AEG asked Peter Behrens to design an advertising brochure for the company's revolutionary new household appliances. Behrens had originally studied painting and in 1897 had been one of the co-founders of the Vereinigte Werkstätten für Kunst im Handwerk (United Workshops for Art in Crafts) in Munich; he was also the director of the Kunstgewerbeschule (School of Arts and Crafts) in Düsseldorf and had already made an intensive study of typography over many years when he was approached by AEG. He removed the ornamentation and embellishment and standardized the numerous variations of lettering for advertising brochures, posters, advertisements, and corporate stationery. The result was a contemporary, businesslike logo and a matching typeface that reflected the trend-setting spirit of the company. Behrens commented: "We register a typeface when reading rather as we notice the flight of a bird or the galloping of a horse. Both have a graceful, pleasant appearance, though we do not recognize the individual limbs of the animal or their position at any one time. It is the overall line that counts, and that is also the essential element in lettering."

In 1907, in the same year in which Behrens co-founded the Deutscher Werkbund (German Association of Craftsmen), he also became the artistic advisor of AEG and as such the very first officially recognized industrial designer. He created a series of electrical household appliances that were inexpensive and easy to use and that convinced with their unadorned, functional design vocabulary. "In design it is not a question of ornamenting functional forms, but of finding forms that correspond to the character of the object and show the new technologies to best advantage," Behrens explained. In addition to advertising material and products, he also designed shop-fittings, showrooms, workers' accommodation, and factory buildings like the AEG Turbine Hall in Berlin (1908–1909), which attracted considerable attention: in short, the entire corporate identity. Thus the comprehensive design language that Behrens developed contributed to the development of a recognizable and unique corporate image for AEG.

What Behrens demonstrated in exemplary fashion for AEG down to the last detail soon caught on generally. After World War II the German electrical company Braun also began to develop a uniform, easily identifiable design vocabulary for its products and corporate communications. In addition to the famous designer Wilhelm Wagenfeld, during the mid-1950s Erwin Braun recruited Hans Gugelot

left—**Dieter Rams, Sixtant SM 31 electric razor** | 1962

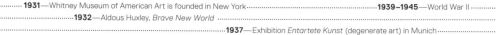

and Otl Aicher from the recently established Hochschule für Gestaltung Ulm (Ulm School of Design). Within a very short time the team, soon joined by the young designer Dieter Rams, succeeded in giving the entire Braun product range a completely new and uniform appearance, and also in redesiging the corporate communications materials, from stationery and advertisements to instruction leaflets. Rams soon became the central figure in the Braun design department, which he went on to lead for 40 years. His products—from record players and electric razors to kettles and other kitchen appliances, as well as hair dryers and calculators—set design standards for clarity and minimalist design. The ideal was optical understatement, sometimes carried through to extremes. Accordingly, the products did not have evocative names but were known by sober alpha-numerical combinations like those previously used by the Bauhaus. The most famous Braun designs included the *SK 1* radio (1955), the *Braun SK 4* radiogram (1956), originally disparag-

ingly referred to as "Snow White's coffin" because of its Perspex lid, the *HF 1* television set (1958), and the *Sixtant SM 31* electric razor (1962, fig. p. 62). The Italian office-machine manufacturer Olivetti and its American rival IBM were undergoing a similar transformation at the same time. Olivetti had a new logo developed in the 1960s and expanded its design department to 100 employees in the fields of product design, advertising, and architecture, with the aim of modernizing and unifying the corporate image. Ettore Sottsass became responsible for product design at the end of the decade, and it was under his direction that the *Valentine* portable typewriter (1969) was developed; it soon acquired legendary status. Like Olivetti, IBM had its old-fashioned corporate image revamped, in line with the company's pioneering role in the field of office electronics and the first computers. Paul Rand developed a new, unadorned corporate logo, which was made more dynamic and modern in the early 1970s by the addition of horizontal hatching.

1943—First New York Fashion Week .... **1958**—Truman Capote, *Breakfast at Tiffany's*... CORPORATE DESIGN **64/65**
........................**1945**—Marilyn Monroe discovered as photographic model ....
..................................**1948**—Jackson Pollock, *No. 5* ....

1949–today Rob Janoff　　**1950–today Zaha Hadid**　　**1951–today Ron Arad**

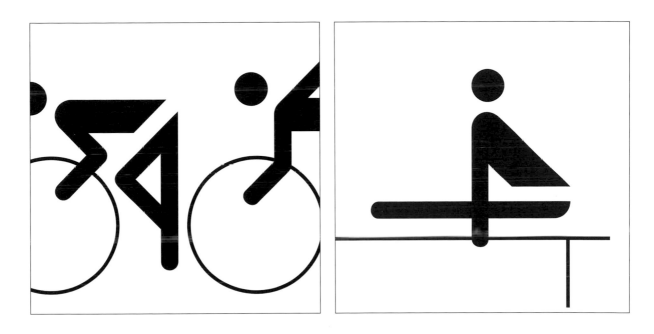

Eliot Noyes designed one of the most attractive office typewriters of the 1960s, the *Selectric* (1961). In the early 1960s Otl Aicher renewed the corporate image of the German airline Lufthansa (fig. left), which has remained largely unchanged to this day. He updated the blue-and-yellow logo with the rising crane, which had been designed in its original form in 1918 by Otto Firle for the Deutsche Luftreederei and which was later taken over by Aero Lloyd. Aicher consciously dispensed with decorative elements and developed a clear, dynamic style for Lufthansa. In addition to the redesign of the logo, he was also responsible for the staff uniforms, the fitting out of the aircraft, and the check-in desks and signage within the airports. Before long many big companies were knocking at the door of the second German pioneer of visual communications. He designed numerous corporate logos, including the Sparkasse logo topped with a large dot, and also his own typeface, named Rotis after the village in the Allgäu in which he lived. Companies like Microsoft, Renault, Nokia, and Audi have adopted it as their corporate font. Aicher and his team were faced with a very different type of corporate-design challenge when they were awarded the contract for the overall design of the 1972 Olympic Games in Munich. Their concept was intended to convey feelings and atmosphere, and it extended from the uniform to the posters and even the entry tickets. The system of pictograms (fig. above) developed by Aicher was revolutionary. It was built up on a simple grid of vertical, horizontal, and diagonal lines. The radically reduced pictograms are easy to understand independently of linguistic skills, culture, or social background. They can be added to at any time on the basis of the strict design guidelines laid down by Aicher; and they can also be used in new fields of application in addition to sports, such as transport. The licensed pictogram system is used throughout the world today in some 900 variants. Aicher thus achieved his aim of creating a new global sign language.

left—— OTL AICHER, LOGO AND PICTOGRAMS FOR LUFTHANSA | 1960s
above—— OTL AICHER, PICTOGRAMS FOR THE OLYMPIC GAMES IN
MUNICH | 1972

66/67 CORPORATE DESIGN ···**1960**—Clement Greenberg publishes *Modernist Painting* ·· **1976**—Apple Computers founded

·····································**1966–1973**—Construction of the World Trade Center in New York ···

···**1970**—British rock band Queen form··

1960–today Karim Rashid   1967–today Jonathan Ive

The harder the struggle for market share becomes, the more important design is in creating a corporate identity that should, if possible, be unique. A current example—and one of the best—is Apple, which, beginning with the legendary Steve Jobs (who died in 2011), pursues down to the last detail a systematic use of the brand and all its products using an exclusive corporate design. In 1976, when Apple challenged the computer giant IBM on the field of home computers, no one would have thought that the little company would one day become one of the big global players. With the *Apple II* (1977), a microcomputer with a plastic casing and color display, Apple developed the first modern, commercially successful personal computer. In the same year Rob Janoff designed the apple logo that continues to be used to this day. From the beginning Apple laid emphasis on user-friendliness and an attractive appearance. In 1984, with the launch of the first "Mac," Apple brought about a revolution. The designer Hartmut Esslinger from Studio Frog Design produced with the *Macintosh 128k* a compact little cube, which, thanks to a mouse and an operating system that made use of the immediate comprehensibility of icons, appealed not only to computer nerds. It was followed in 1985 by the *iMac*, after which the product range was extended in rapid succession: *iPod*, *iPhone*, *iPad*—the elegant designs of Jonathan Ive from Britain convince everyone with their reduced, elegant design and intuitive user guidance (fig. above and right). In a highly regarded ranking of the most important global brands, Coca-Cola was the unquestioned winner for many years. In 2012 Apple challenged the drinks manufacturer for top position as top brand. Apple has accordingly achieved what many strive for: the brand has become an icon. *CH*

above——Jonathan Ive, Apple iPod classic

right——Jonathan Ive, Apple iPad

................**1888**—First issue of the *Financial Times*................ **1907**—Pablo Picasso, *Les Demoiselles d'Avignon*··· **68/69**

................**1891**—Opening of the Carnegie Hall in New York................

1895—First public film screening in Berlin................

1886–1969 Ludwig Mies van der Rohe   **1898–1976 Alvar Aalto**   **1899–1986 Mart Stam**   **1902–1981 Marcel Breuer**

THE CANTILEVER CHAIR: SITTING IN MID-AIR

"I personally have always been of the opinion that a chair is the most difficult everyday object of all to design. You have to recognize how one chair is derived from another and how that one in turn can be traced back to its predecessor. Designing a chair today is no less difficult than building a cathedral." This homage to the chair was written by Mario Bellini, who was referring here to his twin passions as an architect and designer. The metaphor of the cathedral is particularly interesting because it attributes a particular characteristic to the chair as a design object: it can reflect the artistic, technical, and social character of its age. If we look more precisely at the history of the development of the chair, we will find that it also mirrors developments in design in general. In particular, the various materials of which chairs are made are very closely linked with the history of the technology. This applies especially to a very special and unusual type: the cantilever chair.

What is a cantilever chair? According to the dictionary, a chair is an item of furniture on which a single person can sit, and which has four legs, a backrest, and sometimes armrests. But this definition does not apply to the cantilever chair. In a cantilever chair the seat juts out into space; what is more, of necessity it has fewer than four legs. That means that on a cantilever chair the seated person seems to be hovering in space. The best-known form of the cantilever chair is the elegant and comfortable version without back legs, and with a seat that gives slightly when one sits down, so that one seems to be freely suspended. The two-legged chair, in which the elasticity of the material employed is used to the full, reacts to the movements of the person sitting on it and thus permits a gentle springing effect. It retains its stability and does not tip backwards because the resultant energy is diverted backwards via the tension in the front legs and through the runners, which touch the ground. Nowadays an entire range of various designs and materials may be employed. The material that first enabled the cantilever chair to be designed, however, was tubular steel (see *Tubular Steel*). The initial design was the work of the Dutch architect Mart Stam, who presented the first chair with no back legs, made of gas piping, in 1926 (*S33*, fig. left). By dispensing with the support from the back legs, which he realized were unnecessary, Stam was able to make the chair look light, transparent, and

left——**Mart Stam, S33 chair** | 1926

70/71 THE CANTILEVER CHAIR····**1911**····Marie Curie awarded the Nobel Prize for Chemistry ···**1930**····Luis Bunuel, *L'Age d'Or*

·······················**1922**····Discovery of Tutankhamun's Tomb··

···**1929**····The Museum of Modern Art opens in New York··

1926–1998 Verner Panton   1928–today Stefan Wewerka

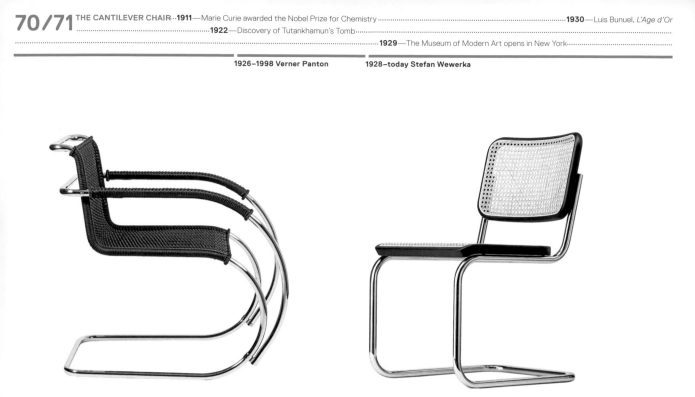

contemporary. With this original example of a cantilever chair, Stam succeeded in transferring from architecture to furniture design the new ideas that dominated the era.

Marcel Breuer and Ludwig Mies van der Rohe refined Stam's design both technically and aesthetically. Breuer had ideal conditions for the study of tubular steel in Dessau, with the Bauhaus's openness to new ideas and its proximity to the Junkers workshops, which provided him with the necessary bending equipment for his furniture experiments. His first innovation in chair design was the *B3* (*Wassily Chair*) of 1925, for which he used runners for the first time instead of chair legs. By doing so he introduced a new approach to the idea of structure in furniture design. The runner, or loop of steel tubing, was also in fact one of the essential prerequisites for the design of Stam's chair without back legs. Inspired by Stam's chair, Breuer then developed his own first cantilever chair in 1928. The models *B33* and *B32* (fig. above right) dating from that year look at first sight very similar to Stam's *S33*; however, as Breuer worked with tubular steel instead of gas piping, he was able to dispense with the unattractive central sup-

port between the front legs. Moreover, and this was the decisive point, in Breuer's chair it was possible to bounce gently up and down. The first true cantilever chair was born.

It was Mies van der Rohe who finally demonstrated how to create a cantilever chair of truly perfect elegance. Unlike his contemporaries he was less insistent on geometric shapes and saw the form not as the goal but the result. His *MR 10* (fig. right) and *MR 20* (fig. above left) have a semi-circular bent tubular-steel frame and a seat of woven cane, which makes them look less technological. In this way he popularized the new form of seating, which became the epitome of modernism. The result was a new feeling of space, which now appeared open and airy rather than solid and monumental. The cantilever chair thus changed not only sitting, but also thinking: people now wanted to float lightly and elegantly into the future.

This objective, and the particular challenge of structure, has continued to inspire designers to the present day. In 1982 the German designer Stefan Wewerka pursued the cantilever principle to extremes. With the oscillating *B5* (fig. p. 73), constructed from a 3.20-meter-long steel tube and with

far left——Ludwig Mies van der Rohe, MR 20 chair | 1927
left——Marcel Breuer, B32 chair | 1928
above——Ludwig Mies van der Rohe, MR 10 chair | 1927

1932—Aldous Huxley, *Brave New World* · 1944—Normandy landings ·

1933—Franklin D. Roosevelt sworn in as president of the U.S. ·

1941—Bruce Nauman is born ·

1932–today Dieter Rams   **1935–today Mario Bellini**   **1939–today Gaetano Pesce**

"Designing a chair today is no less difficult than building a cathedral." Mario Bellini

only one leg, he produced a chair in which it was possible to oscillate in all directions.

The Finnish architect and designer Alvar Aalto rejected tubular steel for his furniture designs, since in his opinion it did not meet truly human requirements. He considered wood, on the other hand, a "form-inspiring, deeply humane material." He had always been interested in bentwood through Thonet furniture, and the cantilever chairs from Germany in particular encouraged him to make an intensive study of the bending properties of wood. He organized timber workshops together with the furniture manufacturer Otto Korhonen, and it was here that *Model No. 31* (fig. p. 75), the first cantilever chair made of wood, was produced in 1931. Taking advantage of the natural moisture in Finnish birch wood, he constructed the frame using laminated birch that had been bent into an elegant arc. The seat and backrest are made of varnished plywood that looks like a sheet of corrugated paper. It lends the wooden chair a futuristic but nonetheless comfortable air. In *Lounge Chair 43* (1937, fig. p. 74), Aalto also succeeded in transferring the principle of the cantilever chair to the horizontal. His designs brought plywood to the attention of the international avant-garde, and in doing so he laid the foundations for a more humane functionalism, as well as Scandinavia's entrance into a new design age.

IKEA's *Poäng* armchair, a copy of Aalto's design, became one of the Swedish furniture concern's most successful products; it has been a permanent feature of the range since the 1970s, and it is available with a variety of different frames and upholstery. Thanks to its low price, it has become a design classic for aesthetes with limited means, making possible design for all (see *Design for All*). Contrary to all prejudices, the workmanship and quality of the chair are excellent, though it is no match for the original with regard to elegance.

Another milestone in cantilever chair design was achieved by Verner Panton in 1967. Like many other designers of his age, he saw the functional and aesthetic advantages of plastics and turned his attention to modeling the wooden cantilever chair he had designed in 1955 out of plastic. It took him five years, however, to find a manufacturer who shared his dream and who was prepared to take on the costs of serial production. The prototype, produced in 1963, was made of fiberglass-reinforced polyester. Research continued with Vitra and BASF, and finally a new plastic (ABS) was developed. In 1967,

right—STEFAN WEWERKA, B5 CHAIR | 1982

1946—UNESCO founded.. 1961—Founding of Amnesty International··· **THE CANTILEVER CHAIR 72/73**

1952—Elvis Presley becomes famous··············

1955—First *documenta* exhibition in Kassel, Germany···

1949–today Beat Frank   **1959–today Tom Dixon**

for the first time in history, it was possible to make a chair entirely of one material and in a single production step. With its sensuous S-curve and its smooth, innovative look, this "chair without legs" revolutionized furniture design and reflected the mood of change in the 1960s. Inexpensive plastic also made the *Panton* chair (1967, fig. pp. 106/107) into a democratic object, by means of which people could firmly set themselves apart from the conservative, middle-class values of the age. The message was similar to that of the tubular-steel cantilever chairs: the person who chose to sit on this chair was a forward-looking individual. And so *Panton* became the chair of that generation and is perhaps the most famous chair design of all time.

Cantilever chairs continue to fascinate designers to this day, a fact that can be seen in the countless chair designs produced by contemporary designers. All three materials described above—steel, wood, plastic—are used. *Myto* (fig. pp. 76/77), the

chair created in 2007 by designer Konstantin Grcic, is of particular interest. Grcic succeeded in producing a new interpretation of the cantilever chair that has already become a sort of contemporary classic. *Myto* was produced in a similar fashion to the *Panton Chair*. Here too a designer (Grcic), a furniture manufacturer (Plank), and a chemical company (BASF) collaborated to develop a new material with particular characteristics. The new material, BASF Ultradur, is an injection-mold plastic enriched with nanoparticles, which make it particularly fluid and stable. It is also non-fading, resistant to cold and heat, and 100 percent recyclable. As a result, the new material permits delicate molding with transitions between thicker and thinner parts, as well as the net-like perforation of the seat, without sacrificing strength. With *Myto,* Grcic has transported the cantilever chair into the twenty-first century and shows yet again that anyone who sits down on such a chair "moves" to the rhythm of the age.

1973—First commercial personal computer .... **1982**—Production of the first commercial cd-player··· **THE CANTILEVER CHAIR** **74/75**

1976—Apple Computers founded ....

1978—The Galápagos Islands are the first item on the UNESCO World Heritage list ....

1974–today Guido Ooms

left——**ALVAR AALTO, LOUNGE CHAIR 43** | 1937
above——**ALVAR AALTO, MODEL NO. 31 (NOW NO. 42)** | 1932

left and above——Konstantin Grcic, Myto chair | 2007

1886—Statue of Liberty erected in New York Harbor · 1903—Kraft Foods is founded · 78/79
1895—First Venice Biennale ·
1900—French Métro is opened ·

1898–1976 Alvar Aalto   1898–1986 Henry Moore   1902–1971 Arne Jacobsen

ORGANIC DESIGN: TAKING INSPIRATION FROM NATURE

In 1940 the Museum of Modern Art in New York launched the Organic Design in Home Furnishings competition. Eliot Noyes, the first curator of the Industrial Design Department at MoMA, hoped that the competition would stimulate the design of home furnishings that "grow out of the many social upheavals," and generate a fresh approach and new forms of expression.

In addition to being awarded prizes and being exhibited, the winning designs were to be produced and then sold in selected shops, led by the New York department store Bloomingdale's. The architects Charles Eames and Eero Saarinen were the outstanding winners of the much-discussed competition, having won in the important categories of Living Room and Chair Design. Their main design was that of the *Organic Chair* (fig. left), a chair with a continuous, three-dimensionally molded seat pan made of plywood, its organic form perfectly suited to the needs of the human body. The jury praised the innovative method used to bend the plywood, but the designs could not be immediately realized because the necessary production techniques and

materials were not available as a result of the USA's impending entry into the war. Production did not begin until 1950, and halted again soon after. The classic design remained dormant until 2006, when it was reawakened by Vitra's first-ever serial production of the *Organic Chair*.

The great interest shown in organic design in the 1940s and 1950s can be understood as a reaction against clinical, cool functionalism and the machine aesthetic, as promoted by the Bauhaus, for example. Geometric lines were replaced by flowing curves. Soft, rounded forms that are adapted to the human body and that are inspired by the multiplicity of forms present in nature characterize organic design, often accompanied by a harmony between form and material. More recently, attempts at organic design have often gone hand in hand with the use of natural materials, such as wood. By the mid-twentieth century, however, there was no perceived contradiction between organic form and experimental, machine-made materials like plywood, fiberglass, and plastic, as the Eames-Saarinen designs show.

Both continued in subsequent years to draw on their designs and ideas for the competition, and developed them further in decisive ways. For another MoMA competition, this one held in 1948 and entitled the International Low Cost Furniture Compe-

left—CHARLES EAMES, EERO SAARINEN, ORGANIC CHAIR | 1940

tition, Charles and Ray Eames designed the elegant, spacious seating-sculpture *La Chaise* (fig. right). With its cantilevered, gently curved fiberglass shell, this lounger is an exemplary piece of organic design, being well adapted to the resting human body. The forms of the *Plastic Armchair* and *Plastic Side Chair* (1950) remained organic, combining formed seat pans of colored plastic with a wide variety of bases.

Saarinen developed an entire series of organically formed seating furniture for Knoll International, including the protruding *Womb Chair* (1946), which promises to engender a sense of belonging equal to that of a mother's body. Saarinen modeled the chair from a plastic shell padded with rubber foam, with loose seat and back cushions. His desire to create a self-contained form led to the creation of the distinctive *Tulip Chair* (1956, fig. p. 82), the seat pan growing like a blossom out of the stem-shaped support. Saarinen had originally intended to make the entire chair out of fiberglass, but concerns over strength forced him to use aluminum for the single leg instead. This was coated with

right—**Charles and Ray Eames, La Chaise** | 1948

1912–1988 Ray Eames   1915–1985 Tapio Wirkkala   1915–2011 Sori Yanagi

82/83 ORGANIC DESIGN···1921—Arnold Schoenberg invents twelve-tone music··· 1929—The Museum of Modern Art opens in New York
1925—Invention of television··························
1928—Andy Warhol is born··········

1926–1998 Verner Panton   1928–today Luigi Colani

polyamide, however, so that it looks as though it is made from one single piece, and the flow of the lines is not interrupted. In his architectural work, too, Saarinen's organic and sculptural formal language is clearly visible, as the example of his TWA terminal for New York's Idlewild Airport (now the John F. Kennedy International) (1956–1962, fig. right) shows. The building, with its domed roof and a flowing progression of walls that appear to melt into the ground, has often been compared to the outstretched wings of an eagle. According to anecdote, Saarinen got the idea for the convex form when he pressed down the centre of a grapefruit rind at breakfast one day, and saw how this caused it to bulge outwards. What could better illustrate the inspiration for his organic designs? Even the rows of seats Saarinen developed specially for the airport terminal are in keeping with the gentle flow of the lines of the building.

The form of organic design that dominated during the mid-twentieth century brought together several traditions. Streamline design (see *Streamline Design*), and later the futuristic Space Age style

of the incipient era of space exploration, created bold lines that developed from the floral lines of Art Nouveau. Scandinavian design, which is closely connected to nature in its forms and materials, clearly also had a considerable influence on designers, including the Finnish-American designer Eero Saarinen. The Danish architect Arne Jacobsen was at the same time creating seating furniture that brought together flowing organic lines and geometric forms. Even the names of his most famous designs—*Ant, Egg, Swan*—shine a spotlight on their models in the natural world. Jacobsen was adept at combining the functional objectivity of modernism with the organic forms of the natural world. In particular his *Egg* and *Swan* chairs, both created for the lobby of the Royal Hotel in Copenhagen in 1958, are all curves and rolling lines, combining the seat, backrest, and armrests into a single, organic form. In the postwar years, the Scandinavians joined the Americans as trailblazers in design. The Finn Alvar Aalto had created a stir as early as 1939 with his Finnish Pavilion at the New York World's Fair. It was approvingly described as a "tremendous wave

left—— **Eero Saarinen, Tulip Chair** | 1956
above——**Eero Saarinen, TWA Flight Center at Idlewild Airport**
(**today JFK**) | 1956–1962 | New York City | exterior view

···**1936–1939**—Spanish Civil War···**1946**—First computer
························**1939**—Germany invades Poland; World War II commences ··
··**1940**—McDonalds is founded··
1939–today Gaetano Pesce

above——**ALVAR AALTO, SAVOY VASE** | 1936
below——**TAPIO WIRKKALA, LEAF-SHAPED WOODEN BOWL** | 1951
right——**TAPIO WIRKKALA, KANTARELLI VASE** | 1946

┈┈┈┈┈┈┈┈┈┈ **1955**—Beginning of Pop Art ┈┈┈┈┈┈┈┈┈┈┈┈┈┈┈┈┈┈┈┈┈┈ **1969**—Woodstock Festival┈┈┈┈┈┈┈┈┈┈┈┈┈┈┈ ORGANIC DESIGN **86/87**
┈┈┈┈┈┈┈┈┈┈┈┈┈┈┈┈┈┈ **1959**—First Barbie doll┈┈┈
┈┈┈┈┈┈┈┈┈┈┈┈┈┈┈┈┈┈┈┈┈┈┈┈┈┈ **1962–1968**—Ludwig Mies van der Rohe, Neue Nationalgalerie, Berlin ┈┈┈┈┈┈┈┈┈┈┈┈┈┈┈┈┈┈┈

1949–today Beat Frank   **1950–today Zaha Hadid**   **1960–today Karim Rashid**   **1967–today Jonathan Ive**

of wood." Aalto was one of the first to turn his back on both the strict geometry of early modernism and also on the use of artificial materials. Following years of experiments, he perfected a technique for shaping and bending laminated wood that allowed him to create curved forms, of which the *Paimio No. 31* chair, the first cantilever chair to be made of wood (see *The Cantilever Chair*), is one example. Designed for the lobby of the sanatorium in Paimio near Turku, the chair was made of laminated birch-wood to simulate the feel of tubular furniture, which Aalto greatly admired. Aalto's perhaps most famous design, the *Savoy* vase (1936, fig. p. 84 above), is both abstract and organic. It was created for a competition held by the Finnish

Karhula-Iittala glassworks, and its wavy form is based on that of a lakeshore. The vases were initially blown into wood molds, which led to slight irregularities in their shapes: a charmingly individual variation of organic design. This came to an end, however, when metal molds came into use in the 1950s.

The designs of Aalto's compatriot, Tapio Wirkkala, were also visibly inspired by nature, with snow and ice, the forests and lakes of Lapland leaving their marks on his designs. Between 1946 and 1960 he created the vase series *Kantarelli* (fig. p. 85), also for the glass manufacturer Iittala. These mouth-blown vases open upwards like a chanterelle mushroom, their fine lines reminiscent of the mushroom's lamellae. A leaf-shaped wooden bowl (fig. p. 84 below) from 1951 may be his most poetic design. Cut from laminated wood, it has alternating light and dark lines which, formed by the thin laminates, perfectly mirror the effect of a leaf marbled with fine veins.

left——LUIGI COLANI, PEGASUS GRAND PIANO | 1990s
above——TERRY DWAN, MAUI WOODEN CHAIR | 2007

The designer Karim Rashid summarizes the trend towards flowing lines as 'Form follows fluid.'

New technical developments included moldable synthetic materials (see *Plastic*) and also laminated wood (see *Bentwood Furniture*) that can be sculpted into curved shapes. These opened up a gamut of entirely new possibilities in design. On example is the Japanese designer Sori Yanagi's *Butterfly* stool (1954), which consists of two elegantly curved plywood elements. Carlo Mollino's *Arabesco* table (1949, fig. right) eschews straight lines entirely, with organically formed sheets of glass resting on a curved openwork plywood frame. Beyond the realms of "high design," the asymmetric form of the classic kidney-shaped table of the 1950s embodies the general population's enthusiasm for free, flowing forms. In the 1960s and 1970s organic design experienced a golden age in numerous plastic-furniture designs. The most famous of these is Verner Panton's cantilever *Panton* chair (1967, fig. pp. 106/107). The first cantilever chair to be made of a single piece of plastic, it combines flowing, expressive lines with a form modeled on the human body and provides a high degree of comfort. Luigi Colani should also be remembered in this context, in particular for his groundbreaking work in vehicle design, which was often influenced by the principles of aerodynamics. Biomorphic forms characterize almost everything developed by this multi-talented designer. Examples include the organically formed headphones for

Sony, the spectacular *Pegasus* grand piano (fig. p. 86) with its ergonomic fingerboard, which Colani designed for the piano manufacturer Schimmel in the mid-1990s, and the *TV-relax* lounge chair (1968), which is reminiscent of a Henry Moore sculpture. The body is made of polyurethane foam, a method Colani adapted from the car-manufacturing industry, and the seat pan is molded from the form of the human body at rest.

In the early twenty-first century, organic design is spreading to virtually all areas of life. A strong tendency towards flowing forms was particularly visible at the turn of the twenty-first century in automobile design. Soft forms are predominant in packaging and product design, too. The designer Karim Rashid summarizes the trend towards flowing lines as "Form follows fluid." Even technical appliances are now characterized by a new, organic formal language in which straight lines, corners, and edges are replaced with curves. This is in large part due to the development of computer programs that make it possible to create designs based on biomorphic forms inspired by nature.

right——**Carlo Mollino, Arabesco table** | 1949

····1769—Invention of the steam engine ·· **1895**—First public film screening in Berlin···

·· **1876**—Invention of the telephone ···

··· **1883**—First motor vehicle with internal combustion engine ························

90/91

DESIGN FOR ALL: THE DEMOCRATIZATION OF DESIGN

There are not many homes that have not got a *Billy* bookcase (fig. left), a *Klippan* sofa, or at least a shoe rack or vase with a melodious name by the Swedish furniture giant IKEA. Over the course of the last 50 years, this company, which has become the biggest furniture label in the world, has shaped the look and feel of our homes like no other with its mass-appeal designs. Its origins are humble, however: in 1943 Ingvar Kamprad founded a small mail-order company in small-town Sweden, selling a wide variety of different products. It was not until the 1950s that he began to sell inexpensive furniture. He stated that he wanted to provide "a better everyday life" for the many. This meant producing shapely, practical, and affordable furniture for all. This idea was not, of course, revolutionary. Kamprad drew on the tradition of Swedish humanism, which aims to create an open and egalitarian society. In this context, design is regarded primarily as a tool used to make everyday life simpler and more pleasant. And so Kamprad adopted the motto of the author and reformer Ellen Key, "Beauty for all" ("Skönhet för alla"), after her essay of that

title published in 1899. "Democratic design for all" (Demokratisches Design für alle) was also the central demand of the Deutscher Werkbund (German Association of Craftsmen) and of its successor, the Bauhaus. The products developed by the Bauhaus were designed to be simple, functional, suitable for mass machine production, inexpensive, and aesthetically pleasing. Despite these goals, avant-garde Bauhaus furniture was in reality far removed from providing design for the masses.

But IKEA's roots reach back beyond these ideas and ideals well into the nineteenth century. It was then that the German carpenter Michael Thonet sounded the death knell for the conventional furniture trade with his bentwood chairs, which could be disassembled for easy transportation (see *Bentwood Furniture*). Like building blocks, the chairs, which consisted of separate parts mounted together, could be combined with parts from other models. In this way, Thonet in the mid-nineteenth century created the foundation for many types and models of industrial serial production. This, in turn, would allow the production of shapely furniture at a low cost, and thus make it affordable for the masses. Thonet also optimized the shipping process: 36 disassembled coffeehouse chairs fitted into a one-cubic-meter crate. The simple design of model *No. 14* (fig. p. 92 right) consisted of five separate parts, which

1907—Deutscher Werkbund founded .... **1919**—Bauhaus founded by Walter Gropius in Weimar ....
1909/1910—Henri Matisse, *La Danse* ....
....**1914**—*Werkbund* exhibition in Cologne ....

1907–1978 Charles Eames   **1912–1988 Ray Eames**

were held together by four screws. By 1930, millions of these chairs had been sold: the prototype of the designer chair for everybody. The low cost of transportation made this chair ideal for export to all the corners of the world, accompanied by advertisements and an annual catalogue that presented the range of products and numerous serially produced models.

The first IKEA catalogue was printed in 1951, four years before the company began to design its own furniture. Its first furniture shop then opened in 1958. In 2012, 208 million copes of the catalogue were printed in 59 editions and 31 languages. Even 50 years later, the approach remains the same: the furnishings and household items designed by IKEA aim to appeal to people through their simple and yet innovative design, their excellent fitness for purpose, and their low price. IKEA furniture is inexpensive not only because it is produced in large quantities, but also because customers themselves

are responsible for two key stages: transportation and assembly. The furniture is unpretentious and easy to assemble, as Thonet's was. As a result, an IKEA design does not make it to the production stage until it can be taken apart, packed in flat boxes, and stacked efficiently in IKEA stores.

From the point of view of design, IKEA has always drawn on classics of design history and on current trends in Scandinavian folk arts. First produced in 1979, the *Billy* bookcase (fig. p. 90) has itself become a classic, with more than 40 million pieces sold. The design was not entirely unprecedented, however. For example, the *T550* bookcase, designed by Bruno Paul in 1908 as part of his *Typenmöbel* (standardized furniture) range for the Vereinigte Werkstätten für Kunst im Handwerk (United Workshops for Art in Crafts) in Munich, appears to have served as inspiration. Similarly, the *Pöang* cantilever chair bears some resemblance to Alvar Aalto's famous cantilever chair *No. 406* (1935). The bent-

1923—First issue of the U.S. news magazine *Time* .... **1933**—Adolf Hitler comes to power··· **DESIGN FOR ALL** **92/93**

1925/1926—Walter Gropius, Bauhaus, Dessau ....

1928—Walt Disney creates Mickey Mouse ....

1926–1998 Verner Panton   1931–today Terence Conran   1932–today Enzo Mari   1932–today Dieter Rams

far left——Ögla chair for IKEA | 1964

left——Michael Thonet, Chair No. 14 | 1859

above and following pages——Furniture from the IKEA PS Collection

from 1995

1938—Pogroms against Jews in Germany .... 1957—Soviet Union launches the first *Sputnik*··· DESIGN FOR ALL **96/97**

1939–1945—World War II

1944—Normandy landings

1934–today Michael Graves   1959–today Tom Dixon

Charles and Ray Eames aimed to provide 'the most of the best to the greatest number of people for the least.'

wood chair *Ögla* (fig. p. 92 left) from 1964 could equally have been part of the Thonet range. The parallels in this case are particularly interesting as IKEA commissioned a former Thonet factory in Poland to produce the *Ögla* chairs, and thus made use of the factory's experience and machinery. The example of *Ögla* also illustrates that IKEA constantly strives for further development and rationalization, however. From 1983 onwards, the chair was made of synthetic materials and could be disassembled, thus reducing its weight and the cost of transportation.

Following decades of relying on anonymous designs, IKEA has shifted the spotlight to its designers. 1995 marked the inception of the IKEA *PS* collection (fig. pp. 93–95), an individualistically conceived luxury line aimed at strengthening IKEA's design credentials. The collection was designed by both newcomers and well-known designers, while—of course—conforming to IKEA principles: low production costs, disassembly for transportation, and assembly by the consumer. The presentation of the *PS* collection at the prestigious furniture fair in Milan proves that the boundary between affordable furniture for the mass market and sophisticated designer pieces is not clear-cut. Some of what is today considered a design classic or expensive status symbol has anti-elitist roots. Just think of the famous fiberglass chairs designed by Charles and Ray Eames. They may be cult objects today, but they were originally created for the International Low Cost Furniture Competition of 1948. New York's Museum of Modern Art sponsored the competition to counter the dearth of affordable, aesthetically pleasing and space-saving furniture. Charles and Ray Eames placed modern designs within the reach of the general population in the postwar years. Following their motto of aiming to provide "the most of the best to the greatest number of people for the least," the designers experimented with a variety of materials to enable large-scale production at a low cost. They eventually executed their design in fiberglass-reinforced plastic. Nowadays, the *Plastic Armchair* (fig. left) is produced by Vitra, with a range of different colors and six different bases, from four legs to the "rod base." It is a good example of the development of new materials and production processes that often accompany the attempt to create an aesthetically pleasing and simultaneously inexpensive design for the many.

left—CHARLES AND RAY EAMES, PLASTIC ARMCHAIR DAX | 1950

1962—Andy Warhol, *Campbell's Soup Cans* .... **1976**—Apple Computers founded ....
1969—Woodstock Festival ....
1973—First commercial personal computer ....

1963–today Marc Newson   1965–today Konstantin Grcic   1974–today Guido Ooms

The *Volksempfänger* ("people's receiver," fig. above) of 1933, in contrast, was created with a propagandist agenda in mind. This radio receiver was designed by Walter Maria Kersting and funded by the Nazi regime. Thanks to its simple form and the inexpensive material, Bakelite, it could be produced for and sold to the masses. It was unveiled at the Berlin Radio Show in August 1933, and more than half a million had been sold by November 1933. The sleek, geometric design—a cuboid housing with a circular opening for the speaker—was entirely in line with the Bauhaus aesthetic, and yet it was first and foremost a propaganda instrument. The *KdF* (an acronym of Kraft durch Freude, "strength through joy") automobile was designed according to similar principles, but was never mass produced. With the help of a savings-card system, it was supposed to make it possible for every citizen to enjoy the use of an automobile. Serial production of what was renamed the *Volkswagen* (the VW, or "people's car") began after the end of the war. The affordable,

robust, and economical VW *Beetle* became a success in the 1950s. Living up to its name, it truly was a "car for the people," becoming a symbol of the German economic miracle.

In Britain, Terence Conran embodied the "Beauty for all" philosophy. In the British class system in particular, good design was virtually unaffordable for the average person at the time. Conran was successful in providing something that was at once trendsetting and within reach of the masses when he opened the first Habitat shop on elegant Fulham Road in London in 1964, selling contemporary interior-design products at affordable prices. He was enormously successful, with his skillful combination of modernism and Scandinavian simplicity,

above—**WALTER MARIA KERSTING, VOLKSEMPFÄNGER** | 1933
right—**MUJI, SECOND TELEPHONE, INDUSTRIAL FACILITIY** | 2005

crafts and "ethno-elegance." In 1992, Conran was forced to sell Habitat, but created a new and successful, if markedly more elitist, chain called The Conran Shop. Conran, who not only designs furniture and home accessories, but also disseminates the principles of good taste via his numerous publications, has became an institution of sorts, a pope of style. He returns to his democratic roots now and again, when he collaborates with his son to design stylish home accessories for Tchibo.

The Japanese Muji chain, founded in 1989, is also dedicated to providing simple, functional and practical products to consumers at affordable prices. The name "Muji" itself states the company's intention: it translates as "no name" or "no label." Muij eschews colorful labels, logos, and unnecessary clutter. It uses in-depth customer surveys to work out what people really need, and puts this into practice in the simplest and most inexpensive manner possible. This focus on the essential is particularly visible in the designs (fig. above). From bicycles to cutlery, the function is highlighted in each product, and everything is reduced and unfussy. Even well-known designers such as Konstantin Grcic and Enzo Mari have created designs for Muji. The irony is that the anti-label Muji has itself become a famous label. *CH*

1883—First motor vehicle with internal combustion engine ⋯⋯⋯⋯⋯⋯⋯⋯⋯⋯⋯⋯⋯⋯⋯⋯⋯ **1903**—First powered flight by the Wright brothers ⋯⋯⋯⋯⋯⋯⋯⋯

1895—Discovery of X-rays ⋯⋯⋯⋯⋯⋯⋯⋯⋯⋯⋯⋯⋯⋯⋯⋯⋯⋯⋯⋯⋯

1900—Boxer Rebellion in China ⋯⋯⋯⋯⋯⋯⋯⋯⋯⋯⋯

100/101

1884–1976 Jean Heiberg   **1904–1972 Henry Dreyfuss**   **1904–1988 Isamu Noguchi**

PLASTIC: FROM SUBSTITUTE TO ESSENTIAL MATERIAL

The word "plastic," deriving from *plastikos*, Ancient Greek for "molded," has long been used to describe sculptural qualities in art. In everyday usage it is usually used as a synonym for synthetic materials, its original meaning forgotten. And yet it is the original meaning that describes the very quality of synthetic materials that is of greatest interest in design: moldability. Synthetically produced substances were at first substitutes for finite and therefore increasingly expensive natural materials, but research and technology have made synthetic materials more and more multifaceted, a development that revolutionized life in the twentieth century. As with automobiles, which have also existed for only about 150 years, it is difficult to imagine a world without synthetic materials.

Most synthetic materials are made from fossil fuels and can be divided into three main categories: thermoplastics, thermosets, and elastomers. Each of these has its own specific characteristics, which are the result of their molecular structures. Thermoplastics, such as polypropylene and polyethylene, can be repeatedly reheated and remolded, whereas thermosets, which include melamine and Bakelite, cannot be reshaped. Elastomers, such as natural rubber and silicone rubber, can be molded using pressure, but then revert to their original shape. They all have strong electric and thermal insulating properties, tremendous resistance, the ability to retain their shape in different temperatures, and a high degree of plasticity. A variety of characteristics and properties can be created through the selection of the material, the production process, and the use of additives. They are therefore ideal for industrial serial production, and provide designers with an almost unlimited spectrum of possibilities.

The foundation of the synthetics industry as we know it today was laid by the American Charles Goodyear in 1839, when he managed to develop a process for vulcanizing rubber. For the first time in history it became possible, through the use of extreme heat, pressure, and the addition of sulfur, to create a type of rubber (thermoplastic) that did not lose its shape in different temperatures. These first "plastics" from the time before 1850 included Goodyear's gum elastic, vulcanite, gutta-percha, Florence Compound, and bois durci (a hard composition made from wood flour mixed with cattle blood and pressed). They were used to make insulation, as well as golf balls, mourning decorations (because they were black, fig. p. 102), hairbrushes,

left—**Charles and Ray Eames, Plastic chair DAW** | 1950

1906—San Francisco earthquake · **1913**—Armory Show in New York shows the European avant-garde · · · · · · · · · · · · · · · ·

· **1911**—Ernest Rutherford develops his model of the atom ·

· **1914**—Marcel Duchamp's first readymade, *Bottle Rack* · · · · · · · · · · · · · · ·

1907–1978 Charles Eames   **1907–2002 Sigvard Bernadotte**   **1910–1992 Acton Bjørn**   **1912–1988 Ray Eames**   **1917–2007 Ettore Sottsass**

hand mirrors, photograph frames, and other richly decorated objects for ornamentation and home furnishings. During this early phase, such items were already industrially produced in small batches. These plastics were used primarily as substitutes for expensive natural materials such as tortoiseshell, ivory, onyx, and mother-of-pearl, and in this way introduced a degree of affordable luxury to the lives of working men and women.

The invention of Bakelite was truly groundbreaking. In 1907 the Belgian Leo Baekeland registered a patent on a process that applied acid, alkali, heat, and pressure to a combination of aldehydes and phenols. This resulted in the first industrially produced, synthetic thermoset. In contrast to earlier plastics, Bakelite could be produced easily and cost effectively, was free of bubbles, had insulating properties, and was very stable. These charac-

teristics, combined with advances in electronics, opened up a wealth of previously non-existent opportunities to designers. During the 1920s and 1930s plastics were improved and their processing methods made more efficient. Large-scale serial production was introduced, such as the manufacture of the *DBH 1001* (fig. right), the Ericsson telephone of 1931, designed by Jean Heiberg. This was the first telephone to have a Bakelite instead of a metal housing. The plastic had better insulating properties and was more hygienic, but, most impor-

above—VICTORIAN GUTTA-PERCHA WATCH CHAIN, NECKLACE CONVERSION | 19th century

right—DBH 1001 BAKELITE TELEPHONE FOR ERIKSSON | 1931

1921—Albert Einstein awarded the Nobel Prize for Physics ⋯⋯⋯⋯⋯⋯⋯⋯⋯⋯⋯⋯⋯⋯⋯⋯⋯⋯⋯⋯⋯⋯⋯⋯⋯ 1936—Charlie Chaplin, *Modern Times* ⋯ **PLASTIC** 102/103
⋯⋯⋯⋯⋯⋯⋯⋯⋯⋯⋯⋯⋯⋯⋯⋯⋯ 1931—Whitney Museum of American Art is founded in New Yorkk ⋯⋯⋯⋯⋯⋯⋯⋯⋯⋯⋯⋯⋯⋯
⋯⋯⋯⋯⋯⋯⋯⋯⋯⋯⋯⋯⋯⋯⋯⋯⋯⋯⋯ 1932—Aldous Huxley, *Brave New World* ⋯⋯⋯⋯⋯⋯⋯⋯⋯⋯⋯⋯⋯⋯⋯⋯⋯⋯⋯⋯⋯⋯⋯⋯

1926–1998 Verner Panton   **1928–today Bernard Quentin**   **1932–1991 Jonathan de Pas**   **1934–today Nguyen Manh Khan'h**

The DBH 1001 was the first telephone to have a Bakelite instead of a metal housing.

tantly, it could be molded into a flowing, ergonomic shape, a fact that would inspire all future models, including Henry Dreyfuss's famous 1937 *Model 302* for Bell.

Bakelite caused plastic to become a symbol of modernity. It was available opaque, transparent, in a variety of colors and white, and its use was not confined to being a substitute for natural materials. The American Streamline designs of the 1930s in particular, including the Hoover vacuum cleaner *Model 150* by Dreyfuss (1936) and the *Zenith Radio Nurse* baby monitor by Isamu Noguchi (1937, fig. p. 185) (see *Art in Design—Design in Art*) increased the value of plastics and made them popular. These designs combined this new, modern material with new, modern forms, producing affordable, well-designed lifestyle articles for the middle classes. The countries drawn into World War II saw themselves confronted with a tremendous scarcity of natural resources, and so governments provided generous funding for research into the synthetic-materials industry. The emphasis then was, of course, on the manufacture of military equipment. It was in this context that the first pieces of Plexiglas were used in airplanes, silicone and rubber in gas masks, and plastics in radio equipment. Development focused on functionality and the improvement of material properties, such as resilience to

wear, temperature change, and aging. This surge in technological advances is particularly noticeably in the visual appearance of products made from synthetic materials before and after the war. Of course the plastics industry in general benefited from the competitive spirit of innovation in various countries. The designers Charles and Ray Eames, for example, designed their revolutionary plastic shell chair (1950, fig. p. 100) from a glass-reinforced polyester that had originally been developed by the military for wheel spats and protective helmets. The result was the first un-cushioned seating furniture made of plastic, with the seat bucket being made of a single piece and manufactured in serial production. The formal language that developed was entirely new, and pushed the possibilities provided by the material to their limits. The products were lighter and more compact, and though the initial cost of development was high, it became lower overall as it was divided up between a large number of units.

Plastics completed their conquest of everyday life in the 1950s. Formica tables, melamine crockery, Tupperware (fig. p. 105), telephones and radios—colorful, inexpensive, and hygienic plastic objects were soon to be found in every household. In Sweden the designers Bernadotte & Bjørn created the mixing bowl *Margarethe*, an aesthetically pleasing

104/105 PLASTIC ············· **1939–1945**—World War II··· **1950–1953**—Korean War

···**1945**—Atom bombs dropped on Hiroshima and Nagasaki ···

···**1949**—Founding of the North Atlantic Treaty Organization ···

1949–today Philippe Starck   **1950–today Zaha Hadid**   **1951–today Ron Arad**

Plastics completed their conquest of everyday life in the 1950s: colorful, inexpensive, and hygienic plastic objects were soon to be found in every household.

and, most importantly, extremely robust and practical household utensil. It was named after Bernadotte's niece, the present-day Queen of Denmark, continues to be produced, and is still a fixture in many kitchens. The postwar economic boom stimulated demand. This had a deleterious effect on quality, however, which finally had a negative impact on the image of synthetic materials. Plastic had become, above all else, cheap and disposable.

Polypropylene, polycarbonate, polyethylene and other high-quality plastics became available in the 1960s. They could be molded into virtually any shape, could be processed in a wide variety of ways, and were very resistant to stress. Social change, the pluralization of lifestyles, and the demand for greater personal freedom were also reflected in design, which became increasingly experimental. These new materials were just the thing. Italian manufacturers such as Artemide, Kartell, Poltronova, and Zanotta in particular encouraged the development of new, unconventional designs, ushering in the golden age of plastic. An unprecedented range of forms, colors, and designs was created. For the first time progressive, futuristic designs were affordable for the general public thanks to the inexpensive material from which they were made. One of the most influential chair designs of all times dates to this period: the Danish designer Verner

Panton's *Panton* chair of 1967 (fig. pp. 106/107). In cooperation with Vitra, he was able to create the first chair to be made from a single piece of poured plastic. With its smooth, sexy, and innovative look, the *Panton* became the iconic chair of its generation. It is at once a plastic sculpture and a plastic chair. The inflatable furniture made from heat-fused polyvinyl chloride (PVC) by Bernard Quentin, Nguyen Manh Khanh, and Jonathan de Pas were also products of this time.

The oil crisis of 1973 put an end to the cheap, cheerful, and colorful Pop era. Plastic was no longer an inexpensive material, criticism of over-consumption and waste gained ground, and environmental awareness was growing. This led, among other things, to increasingly rational designs. A revival of natural materials began, and the image of plastics deteriorated. As a result, artificial materials became, once again, substitutes that were designed to imitate nature, the use of laminates and imitation leather became increasingly widespread.

right——**Advertisement for Tupperware** | 1950s

following pages——**Verner Panton, Panton Chair** | 1967

1954—First commercial nuclear power plant in Obninsk near Moscow ·· **1971**—Founding of Greenpeace ···
··· **1960**—The Beatles form ··
··· **1965**—First Op Art exhibition *The Responsive Eye* in New York ···

1954–today Stefano Giovannoni   1959–today Tom Dixon   1960–today Karim Rashid   1966–today Beat Karrer

The designers of the early 1980s played on precisely this paradox, and rebelled against conservative faux-natural designs. They consciously chose to use affordable, synthetic materials such as laminates, and embellished them with loud, colorful patterns. The Italian design group Memphis was at the cutting edge, not only improving the image of synthetic materials, but also paving the way in the 1980s and 1990s for a renaissance of plastics in design (see *Postmodernism*). Designers thought again about its unique characteristics and made plastic their material of choice. Manufacturers like Alessi hopped aboard the brightly colored plastics bandwagon, having recognized that they were ideal for supplying the mass market, which was in search of designs that were new, modern, colorful, and inexpensive. It was in this context that designs such as the *Bookworm* bookcase by Ron Arad for Kartell (1994, fig. above) and the multicolored housewares by Stefano Giovannoni for Alessi were created. The renaissance of plastics in design was accompanied by tremendous technical developments. In 1998 Philippe Starck created another milestone of chair design with his *Ghost* series (fig. right). These were the first entirely transparent chairs, made from a single piece of polycarbonate in a fully automated manufacturing process. This postmodern design combines historic forms with the most modern of materials and technologies, once again giving plastics an aura of lightness and elegance.

The newest trends in the use of plastic include computer-based designs and ecologically sound designs (see *High-Tech Design* and *Ecological Design*). Many artificial materials are already recyclable, and new types that are made without mineral oils and toxic additives are constantly being developed. Biopolymers, for example, are made from renewable resources like cellulose, starch, and lactic acid. For the company FluidSolids, the Swiss designer Beat Karrer developed a biopolymer from naturally renewable materials and industrial waste products that can be

above——Ron Arad, Bookworm bookcase | 1994
right——Philippe Starck, La Marie chair | 1998
far right——Ross Lovegrove, Cosmic Leaf light | 2009

processed in a wide variety of ways; it is extremely flexible, stable, cost efficient, and itself recyclable. As it can be individually programmed for specific design tasks, it can also be used in a wide variety of ways. In the same way that plastics have in the past contributed to the democratization of design, these new types of plastic could help to make design sustainable. Sophisticated computer programs that can generate three-dimensional models also open up new worlds of possibility for designers using plastics. Forms are becoming more and more complex, and details can be made with increasing precision. Designs by Ross Lovegrove—like the *Cosmic Leaf* light (2009, fig. above right) and the *Ty Nant* water bottle (1999–2001)—push back the boundaries of the ma-

terials and of the techniques with which they are made. Other famous designers whose designs make full use of the technical possibilities available are Zaha Hadid, who is known for her flowing, futuristic forms, Karim Rashid, with his funky, colorful designs, and Tom Dixon, who creates groundbreaking, top-quality, often recyclable products. These modern, futuristic designs are often more redolent of art and sculpture than they are of objects for everyday use, which is what they actually are. Lovegrove himself describes industrial design as the "art form of the twenty-first century" (see *Art in Design—Design in Art*). And that brings us back to the original meanings of plastic: the moldable and the sculptural.

···**1913**—Armory Show in New York shows the European avant-garde ·· **1927**—Charles Lindbergh flies nonstop from New York to Paris···

···**1923**—First issue of the U.S. news magazine *Time*··

···**1925**—F. Scott Fitzgerald, *The Great Gatsby*···

110/111

1922–2011 Richard Hamilton   **1923–1997 Roy Lichtenstein**   **1926–1998 Verner Panton**

POP CULTURE: NEW FORMS OF LIVING

"People get annoyed with you if you like colors. Just as they get annoyed with people with imagination. Most people like things to be familiar. But I have to exaggerate to make my point." With this description of his work, Danish designer Verner Panton hit the nail on the head with regard to a period that rebelled against everything familiar. The 1960s was a decade of change. Various developments in world politics came to a head: the intensification of the Cold War, the escalation of the Vietnam War, student unrest, Women's Lib, and the rebellion of the world's youth against "the Establishment." The resulting general mood of uncertainty stood in direct opposition to an optimism concerning the future, encouraged by the development of new technologies and new materials.

Pop Art, which emerged during this period, became the best-known (and in design one of the most influential) art movement of the postwar years. One of its basic aspects was the attention it paid to the trivial consumer objects of the throwaway society, and it was from this that a dialogue between design and art developed. Artists like Roy Lichtenstein, Andy Warhol, and Richard Hamilton found inspiration in simple everyday objects, and integrated articles of daily use, advertising, packaging, and comics into their artworks. The designers for their part searched for less rigid guidelines than those prescribed by functionalism and good form. Among them, Verner Panton was one of the first to translate Pop Art, with its bright colors, into design. His most famous design, the *Panton* chair (1967, fig. pp. 106/107), was the first cantilever chair made of plastic (see *The Cantilever Chair*). It became an icon of its age for its organic form, its modern material, and its eye-catching color. Designers were inspired by art to make use of techniques such as quotation, collage, and irony in order to develop a new aesthetic for everyday objects. The *Passiflora* lamp (1968, fig. 112) by the Italian Superstudio group is a good example of the integration of comics into design.

The terms Pop Art and Pop Culture were coined during the 1950s and they reflect the growth of popular culture and an ever-expanding consumer market. Art and design were now made deliberately cheaply and were not intended to last. Produced in large editions, the artworks and objects looked witty, sexy, and modern, and they were affordable for the younger generation.

left—JONATHAN DE PAS, BLOW INFLATABLE ARMCHAIR | 1967

·············**1928**—Walt Disney creates Mickey Mouse ·······························

··· **1929**—The Museum of Modern Art opens in New York·············

···**1929**—Stock market crash heralds global economic crisis ·············

1928–1987 Andy Warhol   1928–today Peter Raacke   1930–1971 Joe Colombo

These social changes, artistic ideas, improved production techniques, and new materials, especially plastics (see *Plastic*), sparked off a radical change in design. Reflecting the break with the Establishment, the new design style should accordingly be understood as anti-functionalist and thus as a counter-movement to what had gone before. In contrast to the lack of color and "masculine," rational, geometric forms, now the trend was towards the "feminine," the non-rational, and the emotional. In design this was expressed through organic forms, bright colors, and new materials. The socially critical spirit of the times abandoned reason, the purely utilitarian point of view, and anonymity. A growing longing for freedom, openness, and individualism took over. Designers were inspired by Pop Art, by its bright colors and its curvaceous, often surreal and futuristic forms. The development of new plastics and foam materials, on the other hand, made these new colors and forms possible, expressing at the same time the uncomplicated and casual approach of that generation. The simpler and less expensive production techniques and the spirit of the times also led, however, to a culture of short life cycles and a throwaway mentality.

The brightly colored, affordable designs banished the last memories of the hardship of the postwar era and became a symbol of the optimism of the 1960s. Experimental furniture made of cardboard (*Otto,* 1966, by Peter Raacke), inflatable armchairs (*Blow,* 1967, by De Pas, D'Urbino, and Lomazzi, fig. p. 110), and stackable plastic chairs (*Universale,* 1965–1967, by Joe Colombo, fig. p. 114) invaded living spaces. Beanbag chairs (*Sacco,* 1968, by Gatti, Paolini, Teodoro), cozy flokati (rugs), and hanging seating spheres (*Bubble Chair,* 1968, by Eero Aarnio, fig. p. 115) brought the spirit of liberty and individuality into private homes, because they came free

above——**Superstudio, Passiflora lamp** | 1968

1930—Grant Wood, *American Gothic* ⋯⋯⋯⋯⋯⋯⋯⋯⋯⋯⋯⋯⋯⋯⋯⋯⋯⋯⋯⋯⋯⋯⋯⋯⋯⋯⋯⋯⋯

1939–1945—World War II ⋯⋯⋯⋯ POP CULTURE **112/113**

1936—Charlie Chaplin, *Modern Times* ⋯⋯⋯⋯

1932–1991 Jonathan de Pas   1932–today Eero Aarnio   1935–today Donato D´Urbino   1936–today Paolo Lomazzi   1937–1983 Cesare Paolini

Designers were inspired by Pop Art, by its bright colors and its curvaceous, often surreal and futuristic forms.

from the usual rules governing seating. The furniture series *Up* (1969) became the epitome of the new, conceptual style and new technical possibilities. The Italian avant-garde architect Gaetano Pesce was fascinated by the technique of creating a vacuum and integrated it into the development of his furniture. At its presentation in 1969, the armchair *Donna Up 5*, which was seen as uncompromisingly radical, fascinated all who saw it: each item of furniture was compressed to one-tenth of its original size and vacuum packed in PVC. When the purchaser opened the flat packages at home, the armchair inflated itself.

Two of the most unconventional, creative, and pioneering designers of the era, Verner Panton and Joe Colombo, took the playful experimentation with form and color to new extremes. Both designers were commissioned by Bayer AG to produce futuristic residential units for the Cologne Furniture Fair in 1970 that would do justice to contemporary lifestyles and ideas for living, and at the same time advertise the new synthetic furnishing fabrics. Both rebelling against traditional lifestyles, they combined various functions in a single living area. Bedroom, kitchen, living room, and study were no longer strictly separated; the borders became blurred to reflect the spirit of the times, with its longing for freedom and individualism. While Panton concen-

trated mainly on the new materials and the effects of color on people, Colombo turned his attention to the latest technology and the development of futuristic single-room living concepts.

With his so-called "dynamic items of furniture," Joe Colombo succeeded in creating the future in the present; for this reason he is often described as a design visionary. His modular objects were multi-purpose items of furniture that reflected his optimistic approach to the future. Nonetheless he was always careful to make his designs affordable by keeping the costs as low as possible. He abhorred sharp edges and straight lines and was famous for his organic forms and Space-Age style. The best example is his *Visiona I* interior (1969, fig. pp. 116/117) mentioned above. Here he integrated his pioneering microcosms, the *Central Living Block* and the *Kitchen Box*, which brought together various functions within a very small space in a very efficient manner. For example, in the *Central Living Block* one could sleep, listen to music, read, and watch television, because it combined a sofa, stereo unit, bookcase, and television set into a single unit. Here the individual furnishing modules are fused to form a unique, futuristic "machine for living" that one could imagine inside a spaceship. Colombo's most famous item of furniture, the *Universale Chair* (fig. p. 114), was also employed here. As the

1938–today Andrea Branzi   1939–2005 Franco Teodoro   1939–today Gaetano Pesce   1940–today Piero Gatti   1940–today Paolo Deganella

above——JOE COLOMBO, UNIVERSALE CHAIR | 1965–1967
right——EERO AARNIO, BUBBLE CHAIR | 1968
following pages——JOE COLOMBO, VISIONA I | 1969

name suggests, Colombo wanted to design a universal item of furniture that would combine various functions, and that was made entirely of a single material. After two years of experimentation and research, he finally succeeded in adapting it for mass production. The remarkable thing was that, apart from the rounded shapes and bright colors typical of the 1960s, the chair had interchangeable legs so that it can be transformed in next to no time into a bar stool, a dining chair, or a lounger. The *Universale* therefore really was a chair that could be used in all situations, and it became a best-seller for Kartell.

Verner Panton also designed entire residential units fitted out with his furniture designs. In the process he also created the *Living Tower*, a seating unit that looks more like a sculpture. It consists of two ele-

ments and provides a total of four seating levels. This makes possible a freer lifestyle more in line with the mood of the period. But Panton never limited himself to just one single item of furniture. He established a connection between them and designed the entire room down to the last detail. In addition to the unusual forms, for Panton it is above all the colors that play a central role in design. He enthusiastically studied their effects and was convinced, for example, that our heart begins to beat faster when we see the color red. In his second *Visiona* (fig. p. 118), for example, he plunged into an intensive world of colors. Panton's "living room honeycomb" in strong shades of red and orange are often associated with the uterus and the primordial cell, so that one is mean to feel cozy and safe in the cave-like installation. Panton became the master of

118/119 POP CULTURE ····**1962**—Cuban Missile Crisis ·· **1969**—Woodstock Festival ···························

···**1965**—Beginning of Vietnam War ···

···**1968**—Premiere of Stanley Kubrick's film *2001: A Space Odyssey*······················

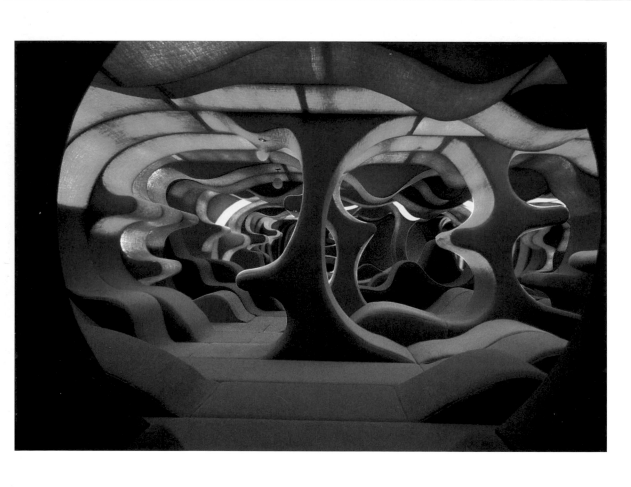

the experimental use of colors, materials, and new technologies, creating not only individual items of furniture that have since acquired cult status, but also unusual living environments that look as if they have come from another planet. The extent of Panton's creativity can be admired in the canteen of the former office building of *Spiegel* magazine, which is now open to the public once more in the Museum für Kunst und Gewerbe (Museum of Arts and Crafts) in Hamburg.

In Italy, the Radical Design movement of the late 1960s and 1970s went one step further than Pop design. It focused on decorative aspects and gave individual artistic elements a *raison d'être*. Among the most important representatives of this trend were Andrea Branzi and Paolo Deganella, with their group Archizoom (1966–1974); and Gaetano Pesce and the architects' group Superstudio, whose best-known design is the *Quaderna* table (fig. right) of 1970, which is covered with plastic laminate with a square pattern. By questioning the fundamentals of functionalism and modernism, Pop design made an important contribution to the history of design. With the "reintroduction" of decor, Radical Design in particular had a considerable influence on the subsequent Italian design groups, notably Studio Alchimia and Memphis (see *Postmodernism*).

above—**Verner Panton, Visiona II** | 1970
right—**Superstudio, Quaderna table** | 1970

............**1911**—German artist group Der Blaue Reiter is founded in Munich ....
....**1914**—*Werkbund* exhibition in Cologne..

120/121

....**1917**—U.S. entry into World War I ....

1888–1964 Gerrit Rietveld	1902–1981 Marcel Breuer	1917–2007 Ettore Sottsass

POSTMODERNISM: DESIGN WITH EMOTION

Postmodern trends in architecture began to emerge in the 1960s in the United States; by the late 1970s designers too began to make reference to historical elements and traditions, instead of attempting to be uncompromisingly modern. They rebelled against the dictates of functionalism and the ideals of modernism, and countered colorless, emotionless, purist, rational forms with colorfulness, irony, individuality, and splendor. The rejection of the old masters is best expressed in the transformation of their basic principles of design: "Form follows function" became "Form follows fun," and Robert Venturi changed Ludwig Mies van der Rohe's "Less is more" to "Less is a bore." In contrast to the similarly colorful and emotional designs of Pop Art, postmodernists combined a variety of styles and formal elements from different eras of cultural history, and celebrated their love of decoration and kitsch. Furthermore, the postmodernists did not demand social change. Their attitudes were much more open, and they particularly enjoyed engaging in provocative acts. They are today considered the trailblazers of the commercialization of emotion.

The Milanese design ensembles Studio Alchimia and Memphis were highly influential in this respect, and went on to have an unexpected effect on the international design scene. Ettore Sottsass, Alessandro Mendini, Andrea Branzi and other designers founded Studio Alchimia in Milan in 1976. It was here that they exhibited their avant-garde objects, most of them unique pieces known as "one-offs." These drew on styles from various epochs, and were considered by their creators as a challenge to classic, functional, industrially produced Italian designs. "Living without planning" was one of Alchimia's most famous slogans. In keeping with the tradition of alchemists, who attempted to produce gold from dross, the Studio Alchimia concept included the use and enhancement of cheap materials. Laminates, plywood, and cardboard were commonly used. The group's exhibitions sometimes made explicit reference to the functionalists against whom they were protesting. At their archly named *Bauhaus I* exhibition (1979), for example, Marcel Breuer's *Wassily Chair* and the *Mackintosh* chair were decorated with colorful little flags and balls, and a cross-shaped backrest was added to Gerrit Rietveld's *Zig-Zag* chair (fig. p. 122). Baroque furniture was also re-designed. Alessandro Mendini's *Proust* chair (fig. p. 123) consisted of a copy of a seventeenth-century chair covered with a colorful

122/123 POSTMODERNISM

····1924—André Breton publishes his *Surrealist Manifestos*·· ·······1937—Pablo Picasso, *Guernica*
··1929—First TV pictures are shown··
···1931—Completion of the Empire State Building by William van Alen ································

| 1925–today Robert Venturi | 1931–today Alessandro Mendini | 1932–today Dieter Rams | 1934–today Michael Graves | 1934–today Hans Hollein |

dot pattern, its form dissolving into a sort of mist. Memphis can be understood as a successor to Studio Alchimia. In December 1980, the 60-year-old Ettore Sottsass brought together a group of young designers, including Michele De Lucchi, Matteo Thun, and the journalist Barbara Radice, to discuss design. Bob Dylan's song *Stuck Inside of Mobile with the Memphis Blues Again* played in the background as they decided to join together to open up new horizons in design. Sottsass, who was at the time already considered the central figure of rebellious, postmodern design, suggested that the group should be called "Memphis" because this referred to both the Ancient Egyptian city and the Rock 'n' Roll metropolis in Tennessee, thus uniting two (very different) eras. The group's first exhibition, at the Salon del Mobile in Milan in 1981, to which other well-known designers of the time such as Michael Graves, Hans Hollein, and Arata Isozaki

also contributed, was a great success. The radical approaches of postmodern design were for the first time recognized as more than mere reaction and provocation: they were acknowledged to be constructive accomplishments in their own right, and the development of a genuinely new style. Sottsass's *Carlton* bookcase (1981, fig. p. 120) was one of the main attractions of the exhibition, and is exemplary of the design championed by Memphis. The colorful bookcase with its four sets of arms is made of laminate and is positioned, like a monument, on a wildly patterned plinth. Sottsass

above——ALESSANDRO MENDINI, RE-DESIGN OF GERRIT RIETVELD'S ZIG-ZAG CHAIR | 1978
right——ALESSANDRO MENDINI, PROUST GEOMETRICA CHAIR | 1978

1939–1945—World War II .... **1956**—Elvis Presley has his first major hit, *Heartbreak Hotel* ....

.... **1945**—Marilyn Monroe discovered as photographic model ....

.... **1951**—J. D. Salinger, *Catcher in the Rye* ....

1934–today Arata Isozaki   1934–1991 Shiro Kuramata   1938–today Andrea Branzi   1939–today Charles Jencks   1942–today George James Sowden

called the pattern *Bacterio* because it looks like a swarming mass of bacteria, spores, and cocci. The design of the time was revolutionized not only by ostentatious appearance, but also by a new relationship between form and function. In the case of the *Carlton* bookcase, for example, form is prioritized over function. *Carlton* is, after all, not really a bookcase; in fact, its form essentially negates the function of the bookcase—it would be more accurate to describe it as a serially manufactured sculpture that invites people to deposit objects on it. The second important break with earlier design was the reintroduction of "decoration," which had until then been a dirty word. The object was now to be animated by colors, patterns, and extravagant forms. One might even say that the piece of furniture itself became a decoration, as its function played only a subsidiary role. The *Carlton* shows clearly how Memphis valued emotional, symbolic, and figurative designs more highly than the anonymous, technical and practical designs of the functionalists.

above—**Philippe Starck, Interior of the Paramount Hotel in New York** | 1990

1961—Yuri Gagarin is the first man in space .... 1973—Premiere of Richard O'Brien's *The Rocky Horror Show* .... POSTMODERNISM **124/125**

.... 1963—Exhibition *The New Figuration* in Florence ....

.... 1968—Premiere of Stanley Kubrick's film *2001: A Space Odyssey*..

Guests entering the lobby of the Paramount hotel feel transported into a modernized Hollywood film-set of the 1920s.

After the first exhibition, Memphis abandoned all of the old rules and set about formulating an entirely new understanding of design. The group was no longer satisfied with the production of one-offs. The intellectual and artisanal approach of Studio Alchimia was considered to be outdated. The members of Memphis wanted to make their bright, colorful, emotional objects accessible to a wider segment of the population. But they simultaneously rejected the dictates of industry and of large manufacturers, considering that these had too great an influence on design. They believed that the limitations of design lay not in the production process, but in the designer. And as manufacturers recognized the great potential of the new, revolutionary designs, they granted the designers this freedom. In this way, the Memphis group contributed to the increased esteem in which designers are held.

The sources of inspiration also became more varied, and the approach to ornament, decoration, color, and material shifted dramatically. Often, mundane places such as bars and offices provided ideas, which in turn were combined with wacky influences from pop culture, comics, music, and television. True to the slogan "Anything goes," they provided striking, provocative, humorous, and ironic critiques of the purist and (for them) sterile aesthetic that had until then been dominant. Now design was allowed, and was indeed encouraged, to provoke emotion. The aim was to create favorite pieces. This emotionality was also expressed in the names given to the objects, which were no longer known simply by numbers or letters. The name became part of the design and told a story itself. The *Colosseum* chair (1984, Charles Jencks), for example, is reminiscent of the Roman monument, the *Plaza* dressing table (1981, Michael Graves) conjures up associations of the eponymous hotel in New York, and the *Murmansk* fruit bowl (1981, Ettore Sottsass) is redolent of the Russian city.

This approach also made possible entirely new sales and marketing strategies. Big companies like Alessi, Vitra, and FSB recognized the potential and began to produce experimental editions. With these editions, which were always created by well-known designers, manufacturers promoted so-called "signature designs," which always named the designer alongside the object, like authors in relation to their books. The Memphis style spread across the globe, and designers became increasingly prominent. Suddenly, Memphis was everywhere. Karl Lagerfeld furnished his apartment in Monte-Carlo with Memphis furniture, all international interior-design magazines reproduced Memphis designs, and pieces designed by members of the group were exhibited in the world's great cities.

1977—Walter De Maria, *The Lightning Field*, near Quemada, New Mexico ⋯⋯⋯⋯⋯⋯⋯⋯⋯⋯⋯⋯⋯ **1986**—Challenger Space Shuttle disaster ⋯⋯⋯⋯⋯⋯⋯⋯⋯⋯

1980–1988—First Gulf War⋯⋯⋯⋯⋯⋯⋯⋯⋯⋯⋯⋯⋯⋯⋯⋯⋯⋯⋯⋯⋯⋯⋯⋯⋯⋯⋯⋯⋯⋯⋯⋯⋯

1982—Production of the first commercial cd-player ⋯⋯⋯⋯⋯⋯⋯⋯⋯⋯⋯⋯

In its early period, postmodern design was often dismissed as pseudo-artistic decoration, condemned as mere silliness and provocation.

International artists, such as Javier Mariscal from Spain and Shiro Kuramata from Japan, also joined the collective.

Popular postmodern interiors include the Royalton and Paramount hotels in New York, which owe their interiors to the French designer Philippe Starck (fig. p. 124). He drew inspiration for the Paramount from French Art Deco, and so it is no surprise that guests entering the lobby feel transported into a modernized Hollywood film-set of the 1920s. A list of the most famous examples of postmodern design, aside from the aforementioned *Carlton* bookcase, might include the *Lido* sofa (1982, Michele De Lucchi), the *Marilyn* sofa (1980, Hans Hollein, fig. right), the *Palace* chair (1983, George James Sowden), and the *Art Deco* chair (1984, Robert Venturi). The *Marilyn* sofa designed by the Austrian architect Hans Hollein for Poltrona combines formal echoes of Neoclassicism and Art Deco with myths from the world of the films and erotic fantasies of the 1950s. The backrest is strongly reminiscent of what must be the most famous photograph of Marilyn Monroe, in which her white dress billows up as she stands over a New York subway grating, and the material of the frame is a reproduction of the polished root-wood so popular in Art Deco. In its early period in particular, postmodern design was often dismissed as pseudo-artistic decoration, condemned as mere silliness and provocation. Alchimia and Memphis were initially met with incomprehension, notably in Germany and the Scandinavian countries, which remained heavily influenced by the Bauhaus, "good form," and natural, organic design. Dieter Rams, for example, criticized the attention-grabbing dressing-up of everyday objects as the "frothing yeast of the Memphis cake." But with time interest in the entirely innovative, surprising furniture designs grew, even there. In Germany there was New Design, which consciously avoided positing new doctrines of style. Unlike their counterparts in Italy, German designers were, however, deeply engaged with social and ecological issues. The designs may feel antiquated nowadays, and are no longer shocking, yet Memphis was indisputably a great cultural phenomenon, and one that caused a fundamental shift in the creative and commercial logics of the world of design. The status of industrial designers also changed as a result of Memphis. Because they imbued their objects with personality, designers became less interchangeable, which meant that they develop a stronger profile; they became part of the design package. Most importantly, Memphis caused design to become more varied, freeing it from adherence to a single value system. Design is no longer static, can evolve unexpectedly, and is allowed to be playful.

........**1989**—George H. W. Bush sworn in as 41th president of the U.S. .... **POSTMODERNISM** **126/127**
.........**1991**—World Wide Web cleared for general use ....
1995—Japanese electronic pet Tamagotchi launched ....

above——**Hans Hollein, Marilyn sofa** | 1980

1923—Sigmund Freud publishes *The Ego and the Id* ·········· **1933**—Adolf Hitler comes to power **128/129**
1925/1926—Walter Gropius, Bauhaus, Dessau ·········
1927—First sound film, *The Jazz Singer* ·········

1923–2002 Angiolo Giuseppe Fronzoni   1928–1994 Donald Judd

MINIMALISM: BEAUTY THROUGH SIMPLICITY

Even in antiquity, the Principle of Simplicity was described as the essence of nature, since nature designs everything in a specific, ordered way that is also the most direct and the best possible way. Minimalism is therefore much more than a style: it is a philosophy that occurs in various disciplines and eras. In art, fashion, music, and architecture—and also in design—there is the same basic approach: a reduction to essentials. In accordance with this definition, today design objects from various decades are characterized as "minimalist." One example is Bauhaus furniture, with its characteristic simplicity of form. The Bauhaus can rightly be seen as a pioneer of Minimalism, though it does not in fact belong to the true Minimalism movement. Minimalism as a design style goes back to a trend in the 1960s and 1970s that embraced all creative areas. Its origin lay in Minimalism in art, which arose as a counter-movement to the use of everyday items in Pop Art. Almost exclusively sculptures, the artworks developed under Minimalism were composed of strongly reduced geometric bodies such as the cube, sphere, and cylinder. It avoided a subjective signature of the artist as well as symbolic, illusionistic, or metaphorical references; it can therefore be characterized as a precisely calculated, rational style that apparently obeyed objective rules.

Although this trend was not able to assert itself properly in design until the 1980s, there had been concepts that translated the principles of Minimalism into design since the 1960s. In 1964 the Italian graphic designer Angiolo Giuseppe Fronzoni was successful with his *Series '64* (fig. left). Fronzoni's designs for chair, table, armchair, and bed were well ahead of their time; indeed, they were not put into production until 30 years later, in the 1990s, by Capellini, and in 1995 they were used for the interior design of the Calvin Klein boutique in New York. The stark cubic forms, the frame of rectangular steel tubing, and the simple color scheme completely in matt white or matt black reflect Calvin Klein's style perfectly. The series made AG Fronzoni a pioneer of Minimalism in design and continued to serve years after its development as inspiration for the works of Maurizio Peregalli, Shiro Kuramata, and Jasper Morrison.

The artist Donald Judd, who had achieved fame in the 1960s as one of the leading representatives of Minimalism in art, also succeeded in transferring concepts from fine art to furniture design. Since

left—**Angiolo Giuseppe Fronzoni, Table from the Series '64** | 1964

130/131 MINIMALISM ···**1936**—Charlie Chaplin, *Modern Times* ··**1945**—Beginning of Cold War

1939–1945—World War II···

1942—Edward Hopper, *Nighthawks*···

1934–1991 Shiro Kuramata

Striving to reach the essence of things, Minimalism attempted to base interiors solely on questions of space, light, and mass.

he was unable to find any furniture for his house that corresponded with his taste, he simply set about designing plain pine furniture himself in the mid-1960s (fig. right). Although the items were intended as unique items solely for his own use, they nonetheless aroused a lot of attention, at least in artistic circles. Together with the small Swiss firm Lehni AG, from 1984 he began producing a series of 15 types of metal furniture, which went into series production. Judd's furniture is characterized by the reduction to the absolutely essential. He used right angles and straight lines as his fundamental elements. Exhibited at countless furniture fairs, it gradually succeeded in attracting the attention of the wider public.

In the 1980s Minimalism in design finally asserted itself commercially. With its purist forms, understated colors, and its use of basic materials like wood, stone, and metal it formed the antithesis of the brightly colored opulence of postmodernism. Inspired by modernism, the International Style, and Scandinavian Good Design, as well as Oriental Asceticism and Zen Art, a style developed based on the idea of radical simplicity. Striving to reach the essence of things, Minimalism attempted to base interiors solely on questions of space, light, and mass. Through the reduction to essential forms, pure beauty, and clear functionality, as much as

possible should be expressed with as few elements as possible. The classic example is the city loft, which, popularized by Andy Warhol's Factory of the 1960s, became the trendy form of living during the 1980s. A loft, mostly an apartment converted from a factory or warehouse, appeals through its clear, monochrome aesthetic. Minimalist furnishings are the ideal accessories for the bare concrete walls, glass surfaces, and steel supports. A loft should radiate a feeling of order by dispensing with everything that is superfluous and by aiming to create a quiet place free of all sensuous stimulation from the outside world.

Minimalist furniture is characterized by straight lines, simple, austere structures, and a lack of adornment. The objects tend to look as if they have been made in a single process. Chairs, for example, usually have no upholstery, and dispensing with superfluous decorative elements means that they can often be stacked or folded away. Shelves and cupboards are often simple boxes that hang on the wall or seem to hover just above the ground. In addition

right——**DONALD JUDD, BOOKSHELVES** | 1966 | unique pieces | manufactured by Donald Judd and R. C. Judd, Die Neue Sammlung, The International Design Museum Munich, during the Judd exhibition 2011. © Judd Foundation

1949–today John Pawson	1951–today Ron Arad	1952–today Ruben Mochi	1957–today Maurizio Peregalli

to using solely wood, stone, or metal, designers sometimes combined these materials with glass or leather. The dominant colors are white, sand, gray, and black; next to these, primary colors are also introduced occasionally so that they stand out against the neutral background. Among the foremost representatives of this period are the designers Shiro Kuramata from Japan, Philippe Starck from France, John Pawson and Jasper Morrison from England, and the Zeus group from Italy. The Zeus group was founded in 1984 by Sergio Calatroni, Roberto Marcatti, Ruben Mochi, and Maurizio Peregalli. In the same year they presented their first furniture collection in Milan, which impressed with its clear geometric design vocabulary. Peregalli in particular concentrated in his early designs on a skeleton-like structure in black. This can be seen in his *Savonarola* chair (fig. left), a new interpretation of a classic chair from the Middle Ages. It is made of black-lacquered, rectangular steel tubing with a seat of black rubber, and it dispenses with all ornamentation. Among Peregalli's most elegant designs are the *Irony* se-

ries (fig. p. 134), comprising a bench, stool, table, bed, rack, and bookcase. Made of phosphate-coated steel, they radiate a cool, unadorned elegance. A number of international designers joined the Zeus group during the course of its existence, including Ron Arad, Andreas Brandolini, Jasper Morrison, and Robert Wettstein. They worked together on an approach to design that was to take over from postmodernism. Among the group's most famous designs, apart from Peregalli's, were the *Anonimus* stools and occasional tables (1986) by Ron Arad, the *Orb* stool series (1994) by Jasper Morrison, and the *Anais Porta Abiti* coat stand (1995) by Robert Wettstein.

Shiro Kuramata, who is considered one of the most important Japanese designers, combines traditional Japanese aesthetics with modern materials and Western elements. Although his best-known items of furniture—such as the clear acrylic *Miss Blanche* armchair (1988), with embedded flowering roses, and the *How High the Moon* S-shaped chest and armchair (1986)—cannot really be described as works of Minimalism, during the 1970s he created impressive minimalist designs in his early works. *Furniture with Drawers Vol. 2* (1970) and the *Glass Chair* (1979) in particular deserve closer examination. In the case of the *Glass Chair*, Kuramata expresses his enthusi-

left——**Maurizio Peregalli, Savonarola chair** | 1984

134/135 MINIMALISM ····**1968**—Premiere of Stanley Kubrick's film *2001: A Space Odyssey* ···································· **2001**—Apple iPod launched

·······················**1980**—Muji founded ·· **1998**—Steven Spielberg, *Saving Private Ryan* ·······················

·· **1995**—eBay founded····························

1960–today Roberto Marcatti   **1965–today Konstantin Grcic**

asm for innovative materials. Here he made use of a newly developed adhesive that enabled him to glue glass sheets together. As the result of the rectangular forms of the sheets and the uniformity of the material, the chair radiates an unusual simplicity. The *Furniture with Drawers Vol. 2* cabinets (figs. right) are also characterized by aesthetic reduction. The remarkable feature of the *Pyramid* cabinet is that it is composed of drawers that are arranged geometrically, whereby each individual drawer is a different size. In the 1980s Kuramata also produced designs for Memphis. In doing so he remained faithful to his Japanese roots and designed objects that were considerably simpler than those of many of the other members of Memphis.

Inspired by Kuramata, the English architect John Pawson also designed minimalist furniture. In his early years in London he was influenced by Minimalism in art; during a long period in Japan in 1973 he became familiar with Zen Buddhism and the culture of simple forms, and met Kuramata. From that point on he followed an austere, cool, aesthetically spare simple approach in architecture as well as in his furniture and interior designs. It was he who in 1995 fitted out the Calvin Klein boutique in New York with Fronzoni's *Series '64*. In his designs, Pawson makes a distinction between architecture, design, and stage set; for him, everything can be traced back to a concern with mass, volume, surface, proportions, connections, geometry, repetition, light, and ritual. In 1996 he summarized this in his book *minimum*, which became an international success.

The fascination of simple, minimalist design continues unbroken to this day. The formal language is frequently no longer quite as severe, and the range of colors and materials has been extended. Successful examples include Jasper Morrison's *Plan* series of chests (1999), Konstantin Grcic's *Chaos* armchair (2001), and Maarten van Severen's *Kast* "storage units" (2005) series.

left——Maurizio Peregalli, Irony Pad Bench
above——Shiro Kuramata, Pyramid and Revolving Cabinet
chests | 1968 and 1970

·············· **c. 1850 BC**—Creation of the Moscow Mathematical Papyrus·· **c. 1450**—Gutenberg invents the printing press ············· 136/137
·································· **AD 105**—Traditional date for invention of paper in China ·····················

870—First codex made of paper in Baghdad ····························

PAPER: A DELICATE MATERIAL WITH HIDDEN STRENGTHS

The use of paper in design has a long history. In Asia it has been popular for many centuries in the manufacture of home fittings. In Japan, for example, it has been used in houses in *shoji*, movable screens mounted with translucent paper; room dividers, lamps, and fans made of paper are also familiar. This is not surprising as the history of paper in the Far East goes back almost 2,000 years. The inhabitants of Ancient Egypt had already discovered a material on which they could record written information: papyrus. But China is the cradle of true paper manufacturing. The first written mention of the art of paper-making dates to the year AD 105. A mulch was made by mashing fibers from the bast of the mulberry tree, hemp, and old fishing nets, with water. This was then drained in a sieve, pressed, dried, and finally smoothed. Buddhist monks spread the art of paper-making throughout Asia over the course of the following centuries. After the Arabs had learned the secret of paper-making in the eighth century, the art spread further, across their vast empire and as far as Spain, and subsequently to the rest Europe.

The construction of water-powered paper mills, Gutenberg's invention of printing with moveable type, and the improvement in the quality (through bleaching with chlorine and manufacture using ground-wood pulp instead of rags, for example), led to a dramatic increase in demand for paper for a wide variety of uses. Prints, banknotes, and packaging were soon a staple of daily life. From the sixteenth century onwards, paper printed with wood blocks was also used for large-scale wall decorations, after the East India Trading Company had brought hand-painted Chinese wallpapers to Europe. The first rolls were used in about 1700, and soon wallpaper began its rise in popularity, later helped by the invention of continuous paper and wallpaper-printing machines at the beginning of the nineteenth century. From the 1830s, wallpaper was omnipresent in the living and sleeping quarters of bourgeois households. Paper in design appeared in a very different guise in the twentieth century, finding its way into Western homes in the unlikely form of cardboard. Designers demonstrated its tremendous versatility, in particular in three-dimensional designs. The fact that it is easy to manipulate and effortless to shape, fold, and cut made it suitable for a wide variety of uses. The translucent nature of paper makes the material ideal for lamp and light manufacture. With his *Akari* lamps of the

left—**Isamu Noguchi, Akari lamp** | 1950s

1644—Start of the Qing Dynasty in China ···································· **1908**—Child Emperor Pu Yi ascends the Chinese throne at the age of two ··············

······················· **1769**—Invention of the steam engine ·······························

································· **1876**—Invention of the telephone ··············· **1928**—Alexander Fleming discovers penicillin·····················

1904–1988 Isamu Noguchi   1929–today Frank Gehry

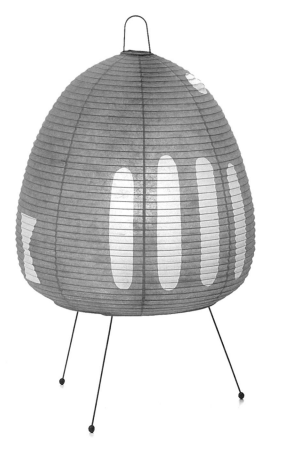

"The magic of the paper transforms the cool electricity back into the eternal light of the sun." Isamu Noguchi

1950s (figs. pp. 136 and above), the Japanese-American sculptor and furniture designer Isamu Noguchi drew on the Japanese tradition of decorative paper lanterns and lights. He created more than 80 "light sculptures," which continue to this day to be produced by Vitra. The paper for his *Akari* lamps is made, in accordance with ancient tradition, from the rind of the mulberry tree, and is then wrapped around a thin bamboo frame. As varied as the shapes are—standard or hanging, simple or ball shaped, elongated or complex geometric forms— they share the same warm, even light. "The light from an *Akari* shines like the light from the sun, filtered through *shoji* paper," said Noguchi: "The magic of the paper transforms the cool electricity back into the eternal light of the sun."

The German lamp designer Ingo Maurer is also fascinated by the medium of paper. In the 1970s he developed the *Uchiwa* series of lamps, using bamboo and rice-paper fans. He played with the design possibilities presented by the material, pleating and crumpling it, and coating it with silver. His *Zettel'z* lamp (1998, fig. right) consists of 49 pieces of notepaper (*Zettel* in German) made of Japan paper, affixed to wires like rays of light around the light source. The pieces of paper are printed with poems

above——**Isamu Noguchi, Akari lamp** | 1950s
right——**Ingo Maurer, Zettel'z lamp** | 1998

and drawings, while blank sheets invite creative input.

Made by sticking or compressing pulp or wastepaper, prosaic cardboard stands in contrast to delicate, translucent paper, which always emanates a certain poetry. It was this unglamorous and mundane material that was used for surprising designs in the late 1960s. Peter Raacke created one of the first pieces of industrially manufactured cardboard furniture in the form of the unadorned *Otto* chair (1966). *Otto* was part of Raacke's *Sitze für Besitzlose* (Seats for the Seatless) series aimed at young people on the move. It perfectly suited the zeitgeist and the sense of new beginnings that permeated the 1960s: the furniture was light, functional, and robust, while the corrugated cardboard simultaneously gave it an air of the provisional, the idiosyn-

cratic, the individual. *Otto* could be used in its original state, but one could also paint it, stick things on it, or varnish it. Nowadays *Otto* can be found in the Vitra Design Museum and the Museum of Modern Art in New York, and it is being produced again in a new edition.

Not long afterwards, the American architect Frank Gehry, best known nowadays for buildings such as the Guggenheim Bilbao, also began to experiment with furniture made of corrugated cardboard. His *Easy Edges* series (1969–1972) was initially developed as shop-window decoration, but soon it was successfully marketed as a commercial product. The items of furniture gain their stability from the use of many layers of cardboard, which are glued together. Gehry's *Wiggle Chair* (1972, fig. p. 140) is particularly notable among the sculpture-like

1971—Founding of Greenpeace · · · · · · · · · · · · · · · · · · 1995–1999—Herzog & De Meuron, Tate Modern, Bankside, London · · · · · · · · · · · · · · · PAPER 140/141

1984—Production of the first commercial cell phone ·

2005—YouTube founded ·

1967–today Tokujin Yoshioka

chairs; elegantly resting on three loops of cardboard, the corrugated-cardboard chair makes excellent use of the material's particular qualities. The arabesque-shaped chair is surprisingly simple in its form, and yet simultaneously robust and stable. In the early 1980s Gehry expanded his cardboard series with *Experimental Edges* (1979–1982). His more recent corrugated-cardboard designs are far bulkier and more spectacular: raw and as though hewn from cardboard, the *Little Beaver* (1980) and *Grandpa Beaver* (1987) chairs built of laminated corrugated cardboard are true seating-sculptures. "What's nice about it is that you can just tear a piece off and throw it away if you don't like it," Gehry himself says about his furniture series. This familiar, everyday material is not always immediately recognizable. The elegantly curved *Cartoons* screen (1992) by the Italian designer Luigi Baroli, for example, is a self-supporting structure made of corrugated cardboard, available in a natural finish or in white. In contrast, the visible honeycomb-structure of the similarly stylishly curved *Wanda* lounge chair by A4Adesign leaves no doubt as to the mundane material from which it is made. This Milanese architecture and design studio is committed to the use of alternative and sustainable materials. Its series of furniture, made entirely of cardboard, is light and yet very stable, thanks to its honeycomb structure. Two meters (6.5 feet) long, the chaise longue, for example, is made from recycled honeycomb-cardboard and felt.

Simple cardboard stools and famous designer pieces made of corrugated cardboard—they all share the air of the uncomplicated, improvised, unfinished.

The aesthetic surprise of cardboard is still present today. From the playful to the geometric, from the simple to the sculptural, the possibilities are almost unlimited. Furniture made from paper and cardboard is inexpensive, easy to make and to transport, stable, and environmentally friendly. It can often be assembled and disassembled in a few simple steps. Through sealing, it can even be made resistant to water and fire. Nowadays, entire offices can be made of cardboard. In 2005 the architects Ro Koster and Ad Kil in Eindhoven in the Netherlands designed an office space for a publishing company and a graphic-design office using nothing but cardboard. Stacked honeycomb cardboard was used to create room-dividing walls around a large, open meeting room. Niches for workstations, cupboards, and shelves were also cut out of honeycomb cardboard. A flame-retardant transparent finish had to be applied to the corrugated cardboard as a fire-protection measure.

The Japanese architect Shigeru Ban has drawn spectacularly on the long Japanese tradition of using paper as a construction material. Since 1989 he has realized numerous projects in which his material of choice was cardboard tube—he was inspired by those used to transport carpets. One of his best-known projects was the 74-meter-long (243 feet) and 25-meter-wide (82 feet) Japanese Pavilion at the Expo 2000 in Hanover (fig. p. 142), its domed structure built exclusively from cardboard tubes. Shigeru Ban is second to none in achieving a balance between functionality and aesthetics. He is

left——FRANK GEHRY, WIGGLE CHAIR | 1972

particularly renowned for his cardboard-tube shelters for the victims of earthquakes in various disaster zones throughout the world.

It is this brilliant mixture of the experimental and the everyday, of the robust and the ephemeral, that makes paper so fascinating as a design material. In recent years in particular, technical advances and inventions such as composites have made paper more durable, more robust and resilient, even to the material's two arch-enemies, fire and water. Using origami folding techniques and computer-controlled laser cutting, designers can dazzle with sophisticated designs that take full advantage of the opportunities provided by the material. Oki Sato's *Cabbage Chair* (2008, figs. right) for the Japanese design studio Nendo is made of a roll of pleated paper that is transformed into a chair by simply fanning out the paper layer by layer; a coating of resin gives the delicate, airy design stability.

It was inspired by the pleated folds that feature in the fashion designs of Issey Miyake. Another Japanese designer, Tokujin Yoshioka, took his cue from natural honeycomb to create his *Honey-Pop* chair (2001). This uses paper honeycomb, which looks fragile at first glance but is remarkably stable, to create a chair that can be unfolded like a paper lantern.

Despite the extraordinary range of materials now available, paper is still at the cutting edge of design.

above—— Shigeru Ban, Japanese Pavilion at the Expo 2000 in Hanover, Germany

right——Oki Sato for Nendo, Cabbage Chair | 2008

1926–1998 Verner Panton

1928–today Luigi Colani

HIGH-TECH DESIGN: TECHNOLOGY BECOMES VISIBLE

High-tech design has no place for ornamentation or decoration. Its products are typically "transparent," with technical details, raw materials, and technical functions clearly displayed. The term "high-tech design" derives from the book title *High-Tech: The Industrial Style and Source Book for The Home* (fig. p. 146), published in 1978. In it, authors Joan Kron and Suzanne Slesin describe a trend in architecture and design during the 1970s and 1980s that chose to make use of materials from industry and technology.

The herald of high-tech design was functionalism, with its motto "Form follows function." Here, for the first time in architecture and interior design, "hard" materials became respectable, used alone or combined with other materials. As in functionalism, in high-tech design the purely functional has an aesthetic. However, "function" is now seen more flexibly, and multi-functionality is introduced, influenced not least by users themselves. From the 1980s commercial goals encouraged the further development of this principle.

A preference for using materials from industry and technology emerged in the 1970s, the aim being to shift the focus of design to an object's function. Until then, the use of hard materials like steel and other metals had been the preserve of industry (such as the defense industry), where the concern is simply with efficiency not appearance. It is to this that designers owe a scientific understanding of the way the materials react under various types of stress, knowledge that they put to good use. Mechanical issues, such as ensuring stability and balance, which likewise derived from industry, also influenced design. In high-tech design, a purpose is given a form, and everything that does not contribute to that purpose is discarded.

High-tech design provides the designer with new possibilities in the range and processing of materials. Through modern production technology, which simplifies manufacture and so reduces costs, it is possible to dispense with expensive and complex processes, and high-tech design takes advantage of this. Just as industry and technology set new standards, so high-tech results in new norms in design. Design becomes the equal partner of technology.

High-tech design makes functional principles from industry applicable in a new context and hence available for use by individuals. Designers

left—RICHARD SAPPER, TIZIO DESK LAMP | 1972

1932—Exhibition *International Style* in the Museum of Modern Art shows contemporary European architecture············· **1944**—International Monetary Fund founded···········

·· **1936–1939**—Spanish Civil War ·································

····················· **1938**—Otto Hahn and Fritz Strassmann discover nuclear fission···········

1932–today Richard Sapper   **1934–today Michael Graves**   **1935–today Norman Foster**   **1943–today Mario Botta**

High-tech places usability at the beginning of any design. What should the object be able to achieve? How will it be used, and where?

make use of this in architecture, interior design, and industrial design. Convenience of use is combined with functionality, which is then presented to the user in a new form. The objects of high-tech design underline the new achievements of technology and combine functionality with aesthetics.

In high-tech design, the focus is squarely on practical objects, but these can at the same time be used to create stylish interiors. The user is challenged to lend them optimal functionality. Design is seen as a link between machines and people. People lend design an individual note, something which functional items were frequently accused of lacking. Industry owes new products to high-tech design, and the economy has thereby acquired a new industrial sector. A new era of design products has arisen through shifting the focus from attractive form to function. This emphasis on functionality means that high-tech design is primarily (though not exclusively) to be found in the office furnishings sector.

High-tech places usability at the beginning of any design. What should the object be able to achieve? How will it be used, and where? One celebrated example is the *Tizio* desk lamp (1972, fig. p. 144) by Richard Sapper. At first sight we might think that what we have here is an oil-feed pump or some other mechanical instrument. Until Sapper launched his design, a typical desk lamp certainly looked very different: there was a clear link between the base of the lamp and the shade, which was mostly round and in the shape of a large reflector (fig. right). The new rectilinear design had no cable, and its balance

seemed questionable. Richard Sapper, however, prefers not to design fashionable forms, since these are "not really original." Fashionable forms are based on previous models, transforming them or presenting a contrast—but that does not make them distinctive or original. In high-tech design it is not primarily design but function that determines the appearance of the object. The *Tizio* lamp owes its appearance to purely constructional and functional considerations. If there are piles of papers and books on the desk—as was the case with the designer of the lamp!—the head of the lamp can easily be moved into any chosen position by means of the flexible pivoting arm. Sapper's goal was free movement through optimum balance, which is achieved by having two arms, each with a counterweight. In order to keep the movement both flowing and free, the precise positioning of the arms enables the designer to dispense with coil springs, which through their tension would force the construction into a specific position (fig. right). The required position of the arms and the angle of illumination can thus be achieved with a light touch, for the *Tizio* represents the interplay of gravity and equilibrium. The design is also innovative because of the lack of cable linking the foot with the head of the lamp. The low-voltage halogen technology permits the replacement of the usual large reflector by a much smaller one, and power is conducted directly via the supporting construction to the light bulb. The beauty of this pioneering high-tech design is the result of the designer's evident enthusiasm for technological sophistication.

............1951—J. D. Salinger, *Catcher in the Rye*..HIGH-TECH DESIGN **146/147**
..........**1954–1962**—Algerian War...
1957—Soviet Union launches the first *Sputnik* ....**1970**—Erich Segal, *Love Story*...............

1950–today Zaha Hadid   **1952–today Matteo Thun**   **1959–today Tom Dixon**   **1960–today Karim Rashid**

Norman Foster, Mario Botta, and Matteo Thun have also turned their attention to the workings of an object and not merely its exterior. The results are industrial products whose forms acquire meaning through their function, which quite often results in a new construction. Thanks to the designers' confident approach, technical solutions to specific problems have become design classics (fig. p. 148).

Nomos (1987) by Norman Foster is a model of high-tech that was intentionally designed to be impressive. It is more than just a multi-functional table (see *Tubular Steel*). The steel-and-glass construction hides the intrusive power cables in the lower part of the frame and thereby ensures that it can attract undivided attention as the versatile focal point of a room. The writing desk can be extended to become a dining table, or it can serve as a projection surface for the slide projector, or it can be transformed into a multi-level working area. In all these forms its uncontested presence is retained, without being intrusive. The slender frame betrays nothing of the physical strength that the relationship of traction and pressure determine, thereby ensuring stability. The clearly visible details give the table the aura of a precision tool. The tabletop

left——Book cover "High Tech: The Industrial Style and Source Book for The Home" by Joan Kron and Suzanne Slesin | 1978

above——Desk lamp with springs and table clamp | 1970s

148/149 HIGH-TECH DESIGN ····1961—Construction of the Berlin Wall ·· **1983**—Production of the first commercial cell phone
··· **1966–1973**—Construction of the World Trade Center in New York ···
·· **1973**—First commercial personal computer ···

1965–today Konstantin Grcic   **1974–today Guido Ooms**

lies on large suction pads such as those also used in transport, and the angular legs recall the powerful but slender limbs of insects. Norman Foster proudly gave his table element the name *Nomos*, in which the Greek work for "norm" can be found. This high-tech item of furniture was designed to set standards, and it achieves this through the demonstrative perfection of its design, and the individualization of the object by the user.

Further examples of this design trend can be seen in Mario Botta's *Prima* and *Seconda* chairs (1982, fig. right). Characteristic here are the use of geometric forms such as the right angle, straight line, and cylinder, the material being lacquered steel. In true high-tech manner, the seat is made of woven-steel sheeting, the cylindrical cushions of the backrest of polyurethane. In the design of these chairs, Botta has remained faithful to his architectural style. Here, too, he is famous for his severely geometric forms, which despite the use of heavy and dense materials like concrete and natural stone still appear light and elegant.

High-tech design looks set to continue into the future. The enthusiasm for the new plastics has prompted many artists to create unusual designs (see *Plastic*). Never before had such a flexible and yet robust material been available for use in production. In 2007 the architect Zaha Hadid designed the *Flow* plant pot (fig. pp. 150/151), which resembles a sculpture. In its asymmetry it recalls the flow of molten plastic; it makes use of the possibilities for creating form provided by polyethylene. Through the progress in computer software, three-dimensional modeling has become possible and the latest technology permits three-dimensional printing. These innovations also contribute to the fact that there are no limits set to creativity and that plastic continues to occupy a prime role in design.

above——ETTORE SOTTSASS, VALENTINE, PORTABLE TYPEWRITER FOR OLIVETTI | 1981

right——MARIO BOTTA, SECONDA CHAIR | 1982

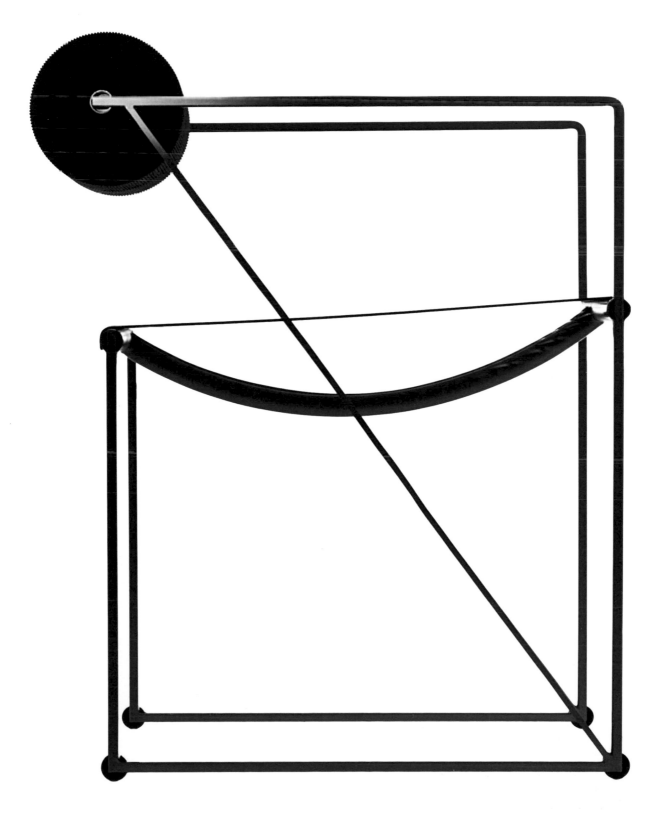

left——Zaha Hadid, Flow plant pot | 2007

1867–1959 Frank Lloyd Wright   1886–1969 Ludwig Mies van der Rohe   1907–1978 Charles Eames

ECOLOGICAL DESIGN: GREEN TRENDS IN DESIGN

Long before sustainability, environmental protection, and carbon footprints became central issues in the design and manufacture of products, a handful of visionaries began to call for a more responsible approach to the use of our planet's resources. Thus the American architect, inventor, engineer, and philosopher Richard Buckminster Fuller (1895–1983) was a pioneer of sustainability and green architecture. From the late 1920s he disseminated his utopian ideas of a better world with the help of futuristic building concepts. In these he reconciled his ecological ideas with his belief in progress and technology. While Mies van der Rohe insisted that "Less is more," so Buckminster Fuller urged engineers and designers to "Do more with less." He hoped that through this principle of minimum effort for maximum performance a design could be developed that produced minimum amounts of waste and excess. In his *Instruction Manual for Planet Earth* (1969), which became the "Bible" of the growing Green movement in the late 1960s, he preached the need for sustainability and synergy.

Two years later the Austrian-born designer Victor Papanek published *Design for the Real World: Human Ecology and Social Change*, which is also now a classic. Papanek, an elective American, was apprenticed to Frank Lloyd Wright. In his book he energetically advocated social and ecological design: design should be inexpensive, environmentally friendly, universally comprehensible, and sensible. "Design must be an innovative, highly creative, cross-disciplinary tool responsive to the needs of men," he wrote; it must "be more research-oriented, and we must stop defiling the earth itself with poorly-designed objects and structures."
Against the background of increasing environmental pollution, the oil crisis of the 1970s, and the consequent awareness of the world's limited resources, Papanek's critical approach to culture and consumerism in the 1970s and 1980s appealed to the mood of the times. After the rift between environmental problems and industrial production had become evident, the environment soon became the concern not just of a minority. Consumers—like designers—recognized that they had an ethical and moral responsibility. In addition to aesthetic and functional aspects, the focus shifted to the complete lifecycle of a product. This included the effects of manufacture and use, as well as the extent to which it could be reused, for example through recycling. Of par-

left——Fernando and Humberto Campana, Sushi IV Chair | 2003

1954—First commercial nuclear power plant in Obninsk near Moscow ·· **1969**—Georg Baselitz, *The Forest on its Head* ··········

1960—Construction of the Aswan Dam starts ··

1963—Bob Dylan records *Blowin' in the Wind* ··········

1953–today Humberto Campana   1961–today Fernando Campana   1965–today Pawel Grunert   1970–today Mia Cullin

ticular importance was the working life of a product, since many of the environmental effects occur while it is in use. Ecological design determines not only a product's form and function, but also its energy efficiency in use. At the same time, attempts are also being made to reduce materials, packaging, and transportation. In addition to ensuring that the extraction of raw materials is as "friendly" as possible, and that production results in few toxins, is energy-efficient, and produces a minimum of waste, designers must also create products that have a long working life and that can eventually be recycled without residues.

Although recycling is not uncontroversial, because it encourages a throwaway mentality, nonetheless what is known as "re-design," which creates products from recycling materials, is one of the most obvious aspects of sustainable design. Nowhere can an ecological statement be so clearly made as in the re-use of obsolete objects and materials, such as PET bottles and industrial waste. Plastic waste in particular, which as a rule cannot be returned to the natural cycle through biological degradation, is ideally suited to re-use. The arc of tension between the starting material and the new product creates interesting connections and contrasts. The appearance of the *B2P* gel pen by Pilot Pen (fig. above), for example, which is made almost 90 percent from recycled PET bottles, demonstrates clearly the parallels with the original product. With its transparent blue casing and the wave-shaped grooved surface, the design of the pens consciously recalls their origins as a plastic bottle.

The Polish interior designer Pawel Grunert uses a different type of recycling. He carries recycling to extremes in his *SIE 43 Chair* (fig. pp. 156/157). The gently curving armchair consists of about three hundred blue shimmering PET bottles held by a slender steel frame, the bottle heads being pushed into a metal grid. Here the starting product has not been concealed; it has not even been changed, but proudly assembled to create an exciting new design item. And if one of the bottles should be damaged, it can easily be replaced at practically no cost!

The idea of creating something new from waste products is very appealing. The *Cabbage Chair* (2008, fig. p. 143) by the Japanese designer Oki Sato from the design studio Nendo has a poetic flair. He

above——B2P GEL PEN BY PILOT PEN

following pages——PAWEL GRUNERT, SIE43 CHAIR

1971—Founding of Greenpeace ⋯⋯⋯⋯⋯⋯ 1977—Walter De Maria, *The Lightning Field* near Quemada, New Mexico⋯⋯⋯⋯ ECOLOGICAL DESIGN **154/155**

1973—First oil crisis⋯⋯⋯⋯⋯⋯⋯⋯⋯⋯⋯⋯⋯⋯⋯⋯⋯⋯⋯⋯⋯⋯⋯⋯⋯⋯ 1978—The Galápagos Islands are the first item on the UNESCO World Heritage list⋯⋯⋯⋯⋯

1974–today Guido Ooms **1977–today Oki Sato**

Recycling is one of the most obvious aspects of sustainable design. The arc of tension between the starting material and the new product creates interesting connections and contrasts.

created an armchair out of pleated paper that is an otherwise useless by-product of certain industrial process. Instead, the sheets of paper are assembled to make a large roll that is then cut into on one side and next unfolded sheet by sheet—like the leaves of a cabbage plant (see *Paper*).

The works of the Brazilian designers Fernando and Humberto Campana, which are multi-layered, provocative, and tongue-in-cheek, seem to blur the boundaries between design, art, and craft. Their "Favela style" is characterized by simple materials of the kind often found on the streets of São Paulo, and designs that typically have an improvised air and the charm of *objets trouvés*. The *Favela* chair (1991) is glued and nailed together from bits of new wood that are always arranged differently. In it they pay homage to the inventiveness of the inhabitants of the slums and shanty towns of Brazil, who—out of necessity—can create something new and surprisingly attractive from waste materials. Since 2003 the chair has been part of the range of the Italian design firm Edra, but it continues to be made by hand in Brazil. The Campanas' chair series *Sushi* (from 2002, fig. p. 152), with its upholstery of densely compressed strips of felt and fabric, rolled up and pressed into a steel frame, is an example of making use of waste products in the best sense of

the word. Many of their works are unique, while others are produced in limited series. When the Vitra Design Museum in Weil am Rhein in Germany presented a major retrospective of their works, the brothers described their method thus: "We give simple objects and everyday items a new life and a new interpretation." It is in this re-use that the ecological idea is contained; no material is too trivial for the Campanas. They used pizza pans to make an occasional table; transformed anti-slip mats into a lampshade; and designed an armchair (*Anemone*, 2001) from plastic tubes. They too transform the improvised, makeshift, hand-made objects that are part of everyday life in Brazil into exciting design ideas.

While the Campanas consciously seek links in their designs between materials by using a collage technique—for example, natural materials like wood or bamboo with plastic or sheet metal—the ideal of ecological design is generally the "monomaterial." This means that the use of various materials is to be avoided, so that re-use and disposal can be effected more easily and quickly, and so that the expense and effort of transportation, and of working with different materials, can be minimized. Ideally, the material should also be a "biomaterial," in other words either a substance that occurs naturally or

1980–1988—First Gulf War .... 1997—Climate conference of the UN adopt the Kyoto Protocol ....

1986—Chernobyl disaster ....

1996—Last nuclear weapons test of France on the Moruroa Atoll ....

1980–today Max Lamb   1982–today Karin Frankenstein

"We must stop defiling the earth itself with poorly-designed objects and structures."
Victor Papanek

that is extracted from natural products, such as biodegradable "no-oil" plastics manufactured from corn or potato starch. The use of unusual bio-materials in particular repeatedly causes a sensation, for example in the *Starch Chair* (2006) by the English designer Max Lamb. It is made of special foam made with potato starch, which is sprayed in threads on top of each other and then solidifies. The result is an eccentric chair that is not only biodegradable, but that could, theoretically, be eaten! Similarly spectacular are the designs by the Swedish designer Karin Frankenstein, whose furniture is formed from a mass of cow dung, scrap paper, clay, and potato flour.

The spectrum of materials used in eco-design ranges from the primitive to the high-tech. *Flower* and *Flake* (2006, figs. pp. 160/161), which the Swedish designer Mia Cullin created for Woodnotes, both consist of small, flat, identical shapes made of Tyvek, a fiber similar to artificial paper that is very strong and has good insulating properties. The tips of these delicate shapes, whose structures evoke snowflakes and flowers, can be joined together in any chosen manner, thereby creating curtains, room dividers, floor coverings, or even three-di-

mensional structures. This versatility as regards possible use is typical of sustainable design.

Last but not least, in the case of ecological design, and especially in the field of technical equipment, it is also a matter of reducing emissions and energy consumption. A good example is the *Airblade* hand-dryer (fig. right), which is particularly hygienic because of its use of innovative technology—the cold airstream is filtered and forced at high pressure through two tiny vents—and which uses up to 80 percent less power than conventional hot-air hand-dryers. Optically, the Dyson *Airblade* appeals for its organic design and a robust casing of polycarbonate ABS.

These creative examples from the wealth of sustainable developments in a wide range of fields serve to indicate that there is currently a clear trend towards sustainable design solutions, which can be easy on natural resources without compromising aesthetics. *CH*

right——DYSON LTD, AIRBLADE HAND-DRYER | 2007

2004—Disastrous floods in Asia .... 2011—Fukushima nuclear disaster .... ECOLOGICAL DESIGN 158/159
2006—A tsunami kills more than 500 people on Java..................
2010—Disastrous oil leak in the Gulf of Mexico ....

left and above——MIA CULLIN, ROOM DIVIDER MADE OF FLAKE ELEMENTS | 2006

1926—Max Ernst, *The Virgin Chastises the Infant Jesus* .... 1946—Salvador Dalí, *The Temptation of Saint Anthony*...

1936–1939—Spanish Civil War ....

1945—Atom bombs dropped on Hiroshima and Nagasaki ....

162/163

1917–2007 Ettore Sottsass   1929–today Frank Gehry   1934–today Michael Graves

SCANDALOUS DESIGN: AT THE LIMITS OF GOOD TASTE

What do a vase in the shape of a penis, a Christmas-tree decoration in the form of a hand grenade, and a coffee service with a pattern based on bloodstains have in common? Nothing, you might think. And yet a more careful consideration reveals that they have a lot in common in terms of a radical approach to design. Breaking away from the customary product world of attractive and functional design, they provoke unusual, challenging, and sometimes even negative feelings.

That permits them to break with the usual ideals of design. While in art provocation has long been established as a strategy, in design it was primarily there to fulfill a particular purpose. Later, when Pop design and postmodernism replaced functionalism, design acquired a new task: to arouse emotions, ideally positive ones. Of course it also aimed to persuade the viewer to purchase a product, and how could that be better achieved than with stylish and attractive objects that prompt an "I want that" impulse (see *Design and Marketing*). But as soon as designers had succeeded in establishing positive emotions in design, it was not long before

some were appealing to the opposite, in other words to negative feelings such as embarrassment, discomfort, even fear or repulsion. And so the objects in this chapter were designed to provoke negative or at least mixed emotions. They aim to challenge and disturb, to provoke the viewer to ask "Why?" In this way a designer can succeed in capturing viewers' attention and arousing their interest.

The reasons for breaching the rules of "good taste" can vary widely. They include protest, the exposure of social wrongs, the breaking of taboos, simple cynicism, pleasure in provocation, or the attempt to break with familiar ideas in order to create something new. However, what lift these designs, and what distinguishes them from others, is the fact that the designer is no longer concerned simply with the aesthetic and the functional, but also with the socially critical. An object will seem disconcerting if it contravenes, questions, or simply toys with our deeply ingrained attitudes and beliefs. However, as the motivation of such designers can be highly individual, and as the objects they create are mostly not self-explanatory, socially and politically motivated design often needs to be explained. Otherwise it is difficult to judge whether a designer is simply tasteless or morbid, or whether, by contrast, he wants to draw atten-

left—Oooms, Roadkill Carpet, detail | 2001

····**1947**—India gains independence from Britain··· **1955**—Beginning of Pop Art··

··· **1951**—J. D. Salinger, *Catcher in the Rye* ···

·· **1952**—Premiere of John Cage's *4'33"* ···

1949–today Philippe Starck   **1950–today Zaha Hadid**   **1951–today Ron Arad**

tion to something in order to provoke thought and positive action.

And just as the designers' motives are varied, so are the objects they create. But some subjects—sex, blood, weapons—recur frequently and therefore deserve separate consideration. The description "scandalous" is applied to much that initially provokes mixed or even negative feelings, particularly when we are uncertain as to how we should react (like Rock 'n' Roll or miniskirts in their day). And since sex, blood, and weapons do not form part of the "normal" design repertoire, they are treated here together under the heading of "Scandalous Design."

Sex, like eating and sleeping, is one of our basic needs. And so it is not surprising that erotic scenes have long had a place in art. So when Ettore Sottsass designed his *Shiva* vase (fig. above) in 1973, he raised the subject of "sex in design." Just as his Memphis group overturned established ideas of good design in the 1980s by questioned everything, so Sottsass did the same by creating a vase in the

shape of a penis. Of course phallic objects have recurred throughout history, and are well known from antiquity and in various cultures around the world; cups with handles in the shape of a penis are not uncommon in sex shops. Here, however, Sottsass, an established designer, was using the penis in so-called "high design." Inspired by a number of trips to India, he designed the vase in porcelain with a flesh-colored glaze and called it *Shiva*, after the god of destruction. Some 30 years later he admitted in an interview with the *New York Times* that the vase still made him laugh. His intention had been that people should take themselves a little less seriously and that the vase should provoke conversation with visitors and lighten the mood.

above——**ETTORE SOTTSASS, SHIVA VASE** | 1973
right——**ALEXANDER REH, FULLY LOADED CHAIR, MADE OF SHOTGUN SHELLS**

·······**1956**—Elvis Presley has his first major hit, *Heartbreak Hotel* ····················· **1964–1975**—Vietnam War ························· SCANDALOUS DESIGN **164/165**

··············**1959**—First Barbie doll ··

······························**1962**—*The Rolling Stones* form··

1959–today Jasper Morrison   **1960–today Karim Rashid**   **1964–today Antonio Murado**

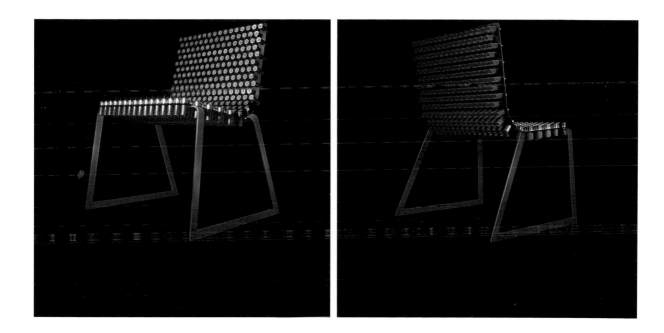

Karim Rashid's use of the subject of sex in his *Karim Sutra* seating units is less obvious, but nonetheless explicit. The American designer, who since the 1990s has been stirring up the design world with his jazzily colorful designs, created it for the New York Museum of Sex. The couch-like object offers—and that is the reason for the play on words involving Rashid's first name—the appropriate position for all 36 different positions of the Kama Sutra. Above all, the seating unit should be fun—whether sex is involved or not.

Blood is sacred in Western culture, a symbol of life; in Judaism and Islam it is a symbol of the soul; and in many other cultures it has mystic associations. Anything to do with blood is therefore always problematic. In 2007 Antonio Murado designed the 14-piece coffee set *Salome* exclusively for the New Museum in New York. But those who sip coffee from the cups and eat cake from the plates may find that the food gets stuck in their throat. For Murado painted the white china with red glaze so that it looks as if it is smeared with blood, thereby shat-

tering that quintessential activity of middle-class smugness, coffee drinking. The artist claims to have been inspired by the bloody legend of Salome. More abstract and yet no less macabre is *Roadkill Carpet* (figs. pp. 162 and 166) by the Dutch design office Oooms, a rug that is based on an animal killed on the road: the gray rug represents the road, the fluffy red patch the pool of blood. The designers Guido Ooms and Karin van Lieshout claimed to have been inspired by a psychological phenomenon that can be observed at accidents: people want to turn away, but feel compelled to look. This repulsion and attraction is heightened by the contrast between the cozy carpet and harsh reality. With their carpet, the two designers aimed to explore the boundary between disgust and fascination. Whether one would choose to put such a scene in one's living room is a matter of personal choice.

Weapons kill. And yet we find them fascinating. Many find them beautiful and admire the precision and craftsmanship hidden behind their cold exterior. So it is not surprising that lovers of

above——Oooms, Roadkill Carpet | 2001

1976–today Pieter Hugo   1977–today Andrew Zuckerman

The reasons for breaching the rules of 'good taste' include protest, the exposure of social wrongs, the breaking of taboos, simple cynicism, pleasure in provocation, or the attempt to create something completely new.

weapons hang the objects of their devotion on the living room wall as in a shrine. But what about the rest of the population? They are more likely to be shocked or alarmed at the sight of a weapon. And why should we celebrate Christmas by decorating the Christmas tree with baubles in the form of hand grenades? According to the British manufacturer Suck UK, which is famous for its somewhat unusual everyday objects, it is above all during the festive season that we should be thinking of the victims of war. Their *XMas Declarations* (2009, fig. p. 168), with the subtitle "6 dead thoughtful Christmas dec-

orations," aims to remind the viewer of war victims; part of the proceeds from sales is donated to Ctrl. Alt.Shift (a Christian organization against global poverty). Here design is clearly being employed to make a political statement.

Much the same also applies to the provocative "weapon lamp" series by Philippe Starck. His *Gun Collection* consists of three lamps: the *Lounge Gun Lamp*, reminiscent of an M16 rifle, the *Bedside Gun Lamp*, which looks like a Beretta hand gun, and the *Table Gun Lamp* (fig. p. 169), based on a Kalashnikov AK47. They are all plated in 18-carat gold,

168 / 169   SCANDALOUS DESIGN   ···**1995**—Japanese electronic pet Tamagotchi launched ········**2005**—*Jyllands-Posten* Muhammad cartoons controversy ················

··**2001**—*Pop Idols* launches the TV casting-show format···

··**2011**—Chinese artist Ai Weiwei unter arrest for two and a half months···

stand on a base, and have a black lampshade. Starck calls on the viewer to reflect on the objects, which is why each lamp is sold with a detailed accompanying document. The latter attacks the global weapons trade, describes weapons as modern icons, and the Kalashnikov, with more than 100 million produced, as one of the most successful industrial design products. The gold of the weapons symbolizes the secret pact between money and war, and the black of the lampshade with its crosses on the inside clearly signifies death. *Table Gun* represents the East, *Bedside Gun* Europe, and the *Lounge Gun* the West. And Starck too aims to do good through his provocative act: 20 percent of the proceeds of the sales go to the association Frères des Hommes Europe Association, an organization for international cooperation whose aim is to help disadvantaged people in underdeveloped countries. Starck removes the weapons from their context, brings them into our homes in the form of a lamp, and thus creates a perfect act of provocation. But however good the intention may be, we find ourselves asking who would really want a weapon lamp in the living room or even on a bedside table—it is hardly likely that a pacifist would do so, and those fascinated by guns might well fail to accept its message.

above——SUCK UK, XMAS DECLARATIONS, GRENADE CHRISTMAS DECORATIONS X 6 | 2009

right——PHILIPPE STARCK, TABLE GUN LAMP | 2005

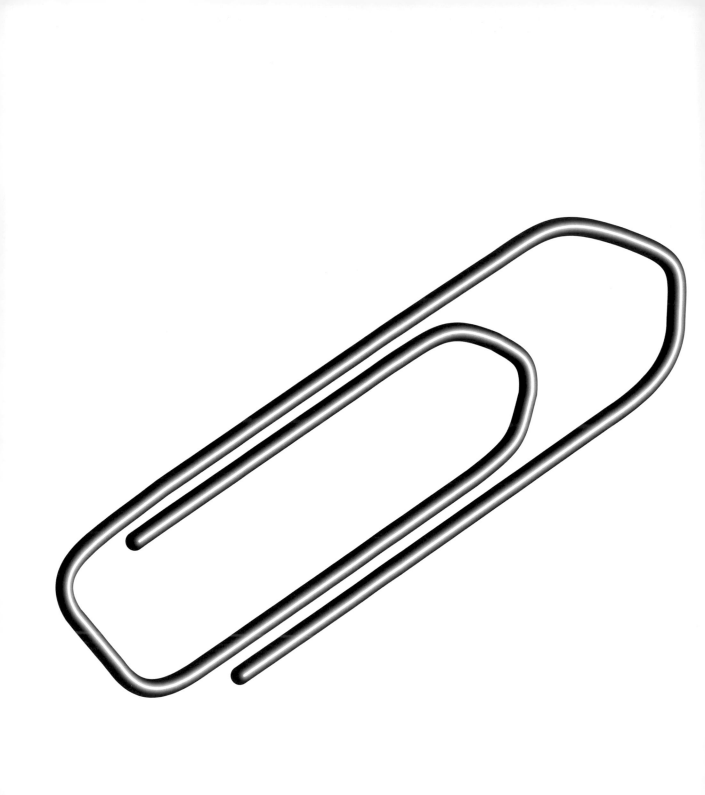

···**1867**—Karl Marx, *Capital*···**1903**—Henry Ford establishes the Ford Motor Company in Detroit ··· **170/171**
··**1876**—Invention of the telephone··
···**1883–1885**—First skyscrapers in Chicago ·······································

BANAL DESIGN: NO-DESIGN DESIGNS

"Banal Design" and "No Design" are terms coined in the 1980s by Alessandro Mendini and Jasper Morrison respectively. Mendini wanted to shine a spotlight on the prosaic objects of everyday life. He and the Italian artists' group Studio Alchimia (see *Postmodernism*) defamiliarized mundane objects and made them new and ironic. They accentuated objects such as clothes pegs, coffee pots, and carpet sweepers by adorning them with decorative elements, thus transforming them into new objects. This can be understood as a rejection of the over-designed, an attempt to draw the consumer's attention once again to everyday objects; it was, in effect, a styling of the banal as high culture. In 1980 Alessandro Mendini, Paola Navone, Franco Raggi, and Daniela Puppa dedicated the exhibition *L'Oggetto Banale* (The Banal Object) to this philosophy. It was this exhibition, which took place within the framework of the Venice Biennale, that coined the term "Banal Design" (fig. p. 172).

British designer Jasper Morrison, a very successful product and furniture designer, was responsible for the term "No Design." He uses it to describe objects that have been designed but do not draw attention to the fact. Of course they include everyday objects, as they did for Mendini, but in Morrison's case they feature simple designs, which have become his trademark. Thanks to the simple, elegant, minimalist appearance of pieces such as the *Air-Chair* (1999, fig. p. 173) and a series of door handles for FSB (1990, fig. p. 174), he became the founder of "New Simplicity" in design. For Morrison, it is the responsibility of design to underline the functionality and simplicity of products through the use of material and form. The everyday use of these objects should feel perfectly natural to the consumer. When asked in an interview how a friend might describe his design, Morrison said only: "Simple." He has expressed the hope that the younger generation of designers will design objects to look unobtrusive, saying that they should concentrate on solving problems through their designs, treating everyday life as their starting point. He and the designer Naoto Fukasawa curated the 2006 exhibition *Super Normal* in Tokyo (figs. pp. 175 and 176). It showcased a selection of 204 everyday objects that pay tribute to simple, straightforward design, from the paperclip and the simple plastic bucket to Dieter Rams's *Regalsystem 606* shelving system of 1960. Morrison and Mendini have been responsible for shifting the focus back to the design of seemingly

left——**PAPERCLIP**

172/173

BANAL DESIGN···**1929**—Stock market crash heralds global economic crisis······················· **1946**—First computer

·························**1936**—Charlie Chaplin, *Modern Times*··

··**1939–1945**—World War II··

1931–today Alessandro Mendini   1945–today Franco Raggi

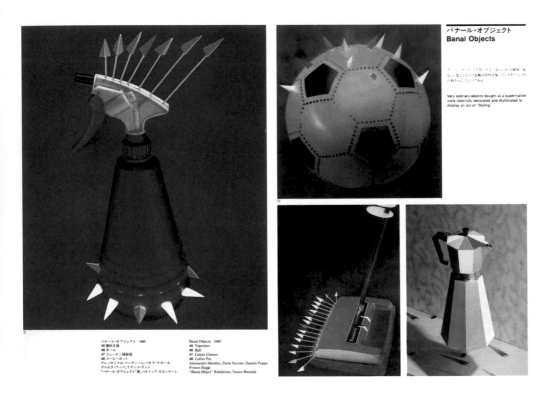

バナール・オブジェクト
Banal Objects

Very ordinary objects bought at a supermarket
were colorfully decorated and illuminated to
display an act of "Styling."

バナール・オブジェクト　1980
45 霧吹き器
46 ボール
47 ジュータン掃除器
48 コーヒーポット
アレッサンドロ・メンディーニ、パオラ・ナヴォーネ、ダニエラ・プッパ、
デニエラ・プッパ、フランコ・ラッジ
"バナール・オブジェクト"展、ベルツィア・ビエンナーレ

Banal Objects　1980
45 Vaporizer
46 Ball
47 Carpet Cleaner
48 Coffee Pot
Alessandro Mendini, Paola Navone, Daniela Puppa
Franco Raggi
"Banal Object" Exhibition, Venice Biennial

banal objects. The roots of No Design and Banal Design reach back much farther, however. The story of the paperclip (fig. p. 177) begins in the mid-nineteenth century, and it will serve as a representative example of the period. Designed as a functional object, its journey from first idea to final product was a long one. In the course of industrialization, new paths opened up for experimentation with materials, and people's ways of working changed fundamentally. Strenuous physical work with heavy physical tools was increasingly accompanied by administration, and thus by office work. This led to a desire for order and clarity in the workplace, and thus to a demand for some of the pioneering objects of Banal Design, such as the paperclip, hole-punch, and file folder.

The paperclip itself reveals nothing about its origins: it has no name or emblem. Its appearance was determined by its inventor, engineers, competitors, and manufacturers. No designer has ever tackled

this innovation, though it did change shape as it matured. First attempts at creating paper holders were made at a time when objects were formed without the input of designers (see *Pioneers of Design*). Businessmen in the mid-nineteenth century demanded new ways of keeping their papers together. Affixing papers to wooden boards using pins, or skewering them on metal spikes, were no longer considered orderly filing systems. The pin developed into the staple on the one hand, shot through the stack of papers using a stapler, and into the paperclip on the other, which does not damage the paper and is reusable. During the 1870 the *Gem* paperclip, which remains unchanged to this day, was developed, alongside a great number of other models. The wire's characteristic double-bend was innovative, allowing it to be opened using gentle pressure and slipped over the paper. The material's tension is carefully calculated so that the clip can be removed with an effortless hand movement,

left——"L'Oggetto Banale" exhibition poster | 1980
above——Jasper Morrison, Air-Chair | 1999

174/175 BANAL DESIGN··**1949**—Mao Zedong founds the People's Republic of China. ······ **1957**—The Treaty of Rome leads to the founding of the European Economic Community

1952—Samuel Beckett, *Waiting for Godot*

1955—Rosa Louise Parks sparks the Montgomery Bus Boycott ·····················

and yet is strong enough to hold papers together. In 1899, an application was made for a patent for a specially developed bending machine to carry out the serial production of this sophisticated design. In this way, the *Gem* model, produced by the English Gem Manufacturing Company, dominated the market. The sliding paperclip was an innovation and became a great commercial success in the world of office supplies.

Other No Design objects also underwent a long process of evolution to achieve formal perfection and functionality. The optimization of the use of materials makes successful imitation virtually impossible. These products have developed out of a need that has been largely fulfilled in the early designs, though they are steadily developed until they reach perfection. From the first time they are used they become essential to everyday life, and are therefore in no danger of falling into disuse. They are frequently perfected through improvements in the materials used to make them, rather than through changes to form or appearance, which are certainly of secondary importance. Machine production cements the product's market position. In the case of the paperclip, rapidly increasing demand even became a barometer of global economic growth. No Design objects are thus largely immune to competition: what, after all, could constitute an

improvement on the original? Perfected functionality can, however, be over-designed with the appearance of a new version, a practice criticized by Mendini. But the imitation cannot knock the original off its pedestal; the function cannot be improved by the new design, which limits the designers' options, and calls into question their *raison d'être*. It is not easy to transform a No Design object into a design object.

Consumers determine the object's life span. For as long as they buy the original, it will triumph over its competitors. Over the course of time, the *Gem* model has undergone some minor modifications, such as the use of thicker wire, colorful plastic coating, and the creation of a corrugated variety, and yet the basic function and form have not changed. Consumers buy such things not because they are beautiful, and not out of a desire for something special, but because they want something that works and that has stood the test of time. This is why they are not prepared to spend a lot of money, and so

above——**Jasper Morrison, FSB 1144 door handle** | 1990
right——**Everyday objects in the exhibition "Super Normal" in Tokyo** | 2006

above——Everyday objects in the exhibition "Super Normal" in Tokyo | 2006

right——Paperclips in various designs

····**1961**—John F. Kennedy sworn in as president of the U.S.·····················**1984**—Production of the first commercial cell phone ·····················BANAL DESIGN **176/177**

1973—First commercial personal computer···

1991—World Wide Web cleared for general use·····················

1960–today Karim Rashid   **1966–today Beat Karrer**   **1977–today Oki Sato**

producers are confronted with a demand for something that is at once useful and inexpensive. The industrial age, and the mass production it allowed, was thus the first period in history during which Banal Design could flourish. Machine production is in fact a prerequisite of the rapid dissemination and popularity of these products. And yet Banal Design objects are, to a high degree, determined by industrial and economic development. Objects such as the paperclip have a specific function, and cannot be adapted if the underlying need changes. They are dependent on social developments and technical innovations. A paperclip continues to serve a purpose only while in the world of work paper is used, gathered together, sorted, and filed. Digitalization and environmental awareness, which continue to grow steadily, will oust paper from the world of work, regardless of the fact that at present that moment appears to be a long way off. But the paperclip is an endangered species.

The social message of Banal Design products is at least as important as their function. Not only do they mirror technological advances (as all innovations do), but they also allow conclusions to be drawn about their users. It does not do to have a chaotic filing system for documents. The paperclip allows the user to file papers in an orderly fashion and to keep together those sheets that, for the user, belong together. We are expected to submit to these unwritten rules governing efficiency. The functions of these objects are apparent even without instructions, and knowledge of their use is inherited rather than deliberately acquired. There are virtually no limits to the social trends and accompanying needs. New technologies, machines, and materials continuously lead to the creation of new objects that can be described as No Design products. What they have in common is this: they are in their simplest incarnations fully developed, and will for this reason remain in daily use for as long as they are needed.

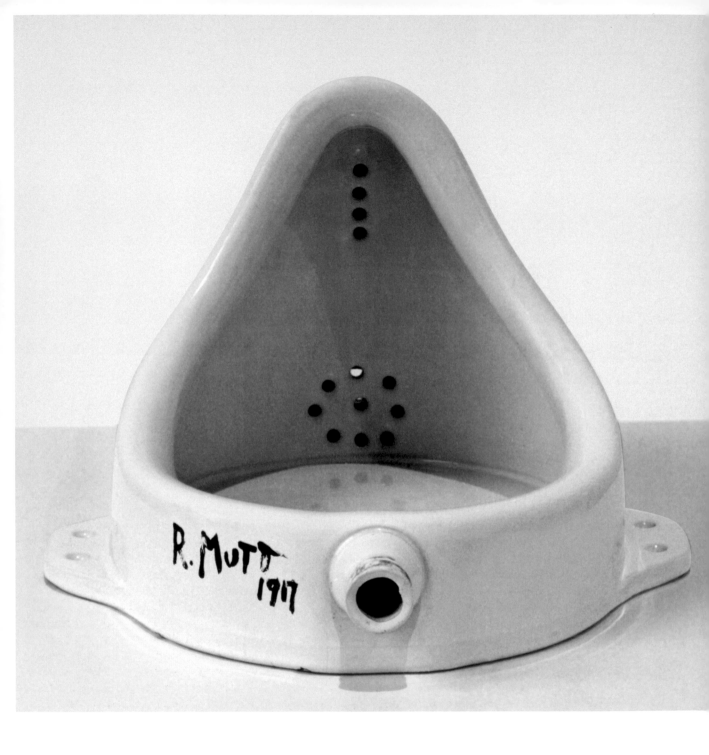

···**1887–1889**—Eiffel Tower built in Paris··· **1914**—Marcel Duchamp's first readymade, *Bottle Rack*························ **178/179**
·····························**1900**—French Métro is opened···
··**1907**—Deutscher Werkbund founded·······································

1887–1968 Marcel Duchamp   **1900–1990 Wilhelm Wagenfeld**   **1904–1988 Isamu Noguchi**

ART IN DESIGN— DESIGN IN ART

Is design art? What is the relationship between the two disciplines? In other cultures, for example that of Japan, no distinction was traditionally made between making everyday objects and making what we now consider artworks. In the West, however, there is a clear distinction between the two. Since the Renaissance, paintings and sculptures have been more highly valued than craft objects: they were seen as representing a purer form of creation, compared with the manufacture of objects with a practical use. And as the importance of the individual grew in society, so artists became famous for their works and began to sign them, enjoying greater prestige; craftsmen, by comparison, mostly worked anonymously. Fine art and applied art thus became two apparently irreconcilable disciplines. Following industrialization, however, design trends developed, especially the Arts and Crafts movement in Britain and then Art Nouveau and the Bauhaus, which once again strove for the unification of arts and crafts (see *Pioneers of Design*). In connection with the new, mechanical production methods, design developed at the interface between art, crafts, and industry.

And as the boundaries between design and art became increasingly blurred, so more and more attention was paid to the design of objects. During the course of the twentieth century, the well-designed everyday object developed into a new genre: the design classic (see *Design and Marketing*). A design classic is a piece of good taste for the home that can be regarded as an alternative to the often unaffordable artwork. The *Panton* chair, Wagenfeld lamp, or Aalto vase have become established as status symbols that provide a form of self-display. Galleries and museums are also reacting to the new importance of design. As early as 1937, a Bauhaus exhibition was held in the Museum of Modern Art in New York, dedicated solely to the works of the design school. There is now a growing tendency to exhibit furniture and paintings together as equals. Design objects are presented in the same way as art.

The expression "design art" is becoming popular. Designers like Ron Arad produce furniture in very small editions of one to ten copies. Furniture is produced that recalls famous sculptures. One example is the *Banquete Chair* (2002, fig. p. 181) by the Campana brothers, an armchair assembled from soft toys, which inevitably recalls American

left——**MARCEL DUCHAMP, FOUNTAIN** | 1917/1964 | porcelain urinal

180/181 ART IN DESIGN ···**1919**—Bauhaus founded by Walter Gropius in Weimar ························· **1929**—The Museum of Modern Art opens in New York

··· **1928**—Walt Disney creates Mickey Mouse ·······································

·· **1937**—Pablo Picasso, *Guernica* ·············

artist Mike Kelley's stitched-together soft toys of the 1990s. Or the lamp series *Weave Your Lighting* by the Korean designer Kwangho Lee, whose interwoven cords stand comparison with installations by the American sculptor Eva Hesse. Marc Newson even describes his items of furniture as "collectible sculptures." It is in this context that one should also regard the record sum of 1.1 million pounds (1.6 million dollars) that Newson's *Lockheed* lounge chair (1986) fetched at an auction in London in 2009. Today, design objects are collected in the way that art is.

Functionalism, which hitherto clearly distinguished items for everyday use from artworks, is no longer the essential prerequisite in design. Here we need only think of Philippe Starck's *Juicy Salif* lemon squeezer (1990, fig. p. 51), which does not even have a container to collect the juice, or Jurgen Bey's *Tree Trunk Bench* (1999, fig. p. 182) for the Droog Design Collective, which is more suited for looking at than for sitting on. Design is becoming more multi-layered; at the latest since Pop design (see *Pop Culture*) and postmodernism (see *Postmodernism*), design has no longer been seen as merely utilitarian; it can also express an attitude to life, convey a message, or aim to achieve a specific effects (see *Scandalous Design*). Design, in other words, has the same function as art.

On the other hand, art too is becoming more varied; it has long consisted of far more than just paintings and sculpture, and has increasingly turned its attention to everyday objects. It was Marcel Duchamp who in 1914 was the first to make everyday objects into art. Nowadays no one is surprised to find mundane items of everyday use in a museum, but his *Bottle Drier* (1914) and *Fountain* (1917, fig. p. 178) were shocking when first exhibited. Viewers were astonished to see such prosaic objects in an art museum, because both sculptures, known today as ready-mades, are ordinary everyday objects, namely a bottle drier and a urinal, that the artist merely placed on a plinth, signed, and thereby elevated to the realm of art. Until that point, art was always supposed to be meaningful and the result of skill. Duchamp rejected these ideas. For him the artistic act lay in the selection of the object. Making them visible, and granting them an aesthetic significance, Duchamp transformed everyday items (design) into art. Duchamp's ready-mades are among the key

right——**Fernando and Humberto Campana, Banquete Chair** | 2002

above——JURGEN BEY FOR DROOG, TREE TRUNK BENCH | 1999

···**1941**—Bruce Nauman is born ··· **1955**—Beginning of Pop Art ··· ART IN DESIGN **182/183**

···········**1942**—Edward Hopper, *Nighthawks*···

·· **1960**—Clement Greenberg publishes *Modernist Painting* ···················

1944–today Hartmut Esslinger   **1954–2012 Mike Kelley**

works of modern art and paved the way for assemblage and Concept Art, and later also for Pop Art, which focused specifically on everyday objects (see *Pop Culture*).

Richard Artschwager also operated at the interface between art and design. After working as a designer for a New York furniture manufacturer during the 1950s, in the 1960s he began to examine the perceptible barriers between art and design. His *Table and Chair* of 1962/1963, as well as his *Chair* of 1963, can be described as crossovers between art and design, and between picture and object. They were sculptures that could be used as furniture, but as furniture they were only noticeable for their painted surfaces. Artschwager himself commented: "I wanted to create a sculpture for looking at and a painting to grasp hold of." Artschwager made the crossover of disciplines an aesthetic principle.

Fascinated by three-dimensional structures, Isamu Noguchi also moved freely between the disciplines as a sculptor, product designer, stage designer, and landscape architect. He exhibited his works, for example, at the documenta in Kassel (1959 and 1964) and the Biennale in Venice (1986); designed the famous *Akari* paper light fittings (see *Paper*, figs. pp. 136 and 138) and the *Zenith Radio Nurse* a baby monitor (1937, fig. p. 185); created

stage designs for dance theatres in New York; made sculptures like the *Garden Seat* (1963) and *Water Table* (1968, fig. p. 184), which invite the viewer to use them; and designed a number of large gardens, including the UNESCO garden in Paris. His special sense of clear aesthetics runs like a golden thread through all his works, and he did not distinguish between creating a table, a sculpture, or a stage set.

With his installation in the café at the Biennale in Venice in 2009 (fig. pp. 186/187), German conceptual artist Tobias Rehberger also achieved a symbiosis of art and design. He purposely designed a space that would not be primarily visited because of the art; he wanted to create an artwork for people to experience. The eye-catching color scheme (with its strong contrasts of white, black, yellow, and red), the mirror installations, and the strong geometric motifs cause confusion, and not only optically. Can a functional room like a café be art? His receiving the Golden Lion for Best Artist award, one of the world's most prestigious art prizes, can perhaps serve as an answer here. Rehberger himself said of the relationship between design and art: "There is no difference which one can distinguish from the outside." And so it is scarcely surprising that his tables, lamps, and benches, which he designed specially for the ex-

1966—Barnett Newman, *Who's Afraid of Red, Yellow and Blue* .... **1977–1980**—Cindy Sherman produces *Untitled Film Stills* ....

1968—Premiere of Stanley Kubrick's film *2001: A Space Odyssey* ....

1970—Robert Smithson, *Spiral Jetty*, Great Salt Lake, Utah ....

1961–today Fernando Campana   1963–today Marc Newson   1966–today Tobias Rehberger   1967–today Kwangho Lee

hibition, should be featured in art publications as well as in those relating to design and interiors. The differentiation between art and design becomes progressively more problematic, because objects no longer possess obvious characteristics that would classify them clearly as the one or the other. Art makes use of design in the same way as design makes use of art. Nor does the institutional connection via the gallery or museum seem to be essential today, so we must ask ourselves whether a strict differentiation is necessary at all. There does, however, seem to be one decisive parameter: while the artist is mostly free in his creative work, the designer is largely bound by the terms of the client's brief. And whereas good design is most certainly (an) art, we should nonetheless end the discussion on design and art with Hartmut Esslinger's pragmatic assertion: "Design has nothing to do with art. Design is a service."

above——ISAMO NOGUCHI, WATER TABLE | 1968
right——ISAMO NOGUCHI, ZENITH RADIO NURSE BABY MONITOR | 1937
following pages——TOBIAS REHBERGER, WHAT YOU LOVE ALSO MAKES YOU CRY | 2009 | Installation in the Palazzo delle Esposizioni at the Venice Biennale

1986—Jeff Koons, *Rabbit* .... **1995–1999**—Herzog & De Meuron, Tate Modern, Bankside, London .... **ART IN DESIGN** **184/185**

............**1988**—*Freeze* exhibition shows the Young British Artists in London ....

2011—Chinese artist Ai Weiwei under arrest for two and a half months ....

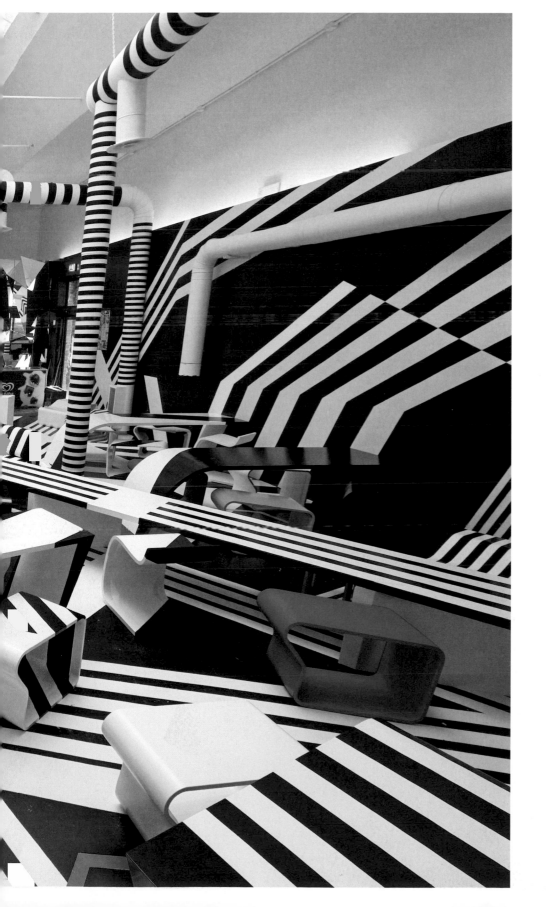

DESIGNERS AND ARTISTS

Alvar **Aalto**: * 3 February 1898 in Kuortane, Finland; † 11 May 1976 in Helsinki

Eero **Aarnio**: * 21 July 1932 in Helsinki

Otl (Otto) **Aicher**: * 13 May 1922 in Ulm, Germany; † 1 September 1991 in Günzburg, Germany

Ron **Arad**: * 1951 in Tel Aviv, Israel

Richard **Artschwager**: * 26 December 1923 in Washington, DC; † 9 February 2013 in Albany, New York

Peter **Behrens**: * 14 April 1868 in Hamburg; † 27 February 1940 in Berlin

Norman **Bel Geddes**: * 27 April 1893 in Adrian, Michigan; † 8 May 1958 in New York

Mario **Bellini**: * 1 February 1935 in Milan

Sigvard **Bernadotte**: * 7 June 1907 at Drottningholm Palace, Sweden; † 4 February 2002 in Stockholm

Max **Bill**: * 22 December 1908 in Winterthur, Switzerland; † 9 December 1994 in Berlin

Acton **Bjørn**: * 23 September 1910 in Copenhagen; † 20 June 1992 in Charlottenlund, Denmark

Mario **Botta**: * 1 April 1943 in Mendrisio, Switzerland

Andreas **Brandolini**: * 21 August 1951 in Taucha, Germany

Andrea **Branzi**: * 1938 in Florence

Marcel **Breuer**: * 21 May 1902 in Fünfkirchen, Austria-Hungary (today Pécs, Hungary); † 1 July 1981 in New York

Richard **Buckminster Fuller**: * 12 July 1895 in Milton, Massachusetts, † 1 July 1983 in Los Angeles

Sergio **Calatroni**: * 1951 in Santa Giuletta, Italy

Fernando **Campana**: * 19 May 1961 in Brotas, Brazil

Humberto **Campana**: * 17 March 1953 in Rio Claro, Brazil

Luigi **Colani**: * 2 August 1928 in Berlin

Joe **Colombo**: * 30 July 1930 in Milan; † 30 July 1971 in Milan

Mia **Cullin**: * 1970 in Lund, Sweden

Paolo **Deganello**: * 1940 in Este, Italy

Michele **De Lucchi**: * 8 November 1951 in Ferrara, Italy

Jonathan **De Pas**: * 1932 in Milan; † 1991

Donald **Deskey**: * 23 November 1894 in Blue Earth, Minnesota; † 29 April 1989 in Vero Beach, Florida

Erich **Dieckmann**: * 1896 in Kauernik (today Kurzętnik, Poland); † 1944 in Berlin

Tom **Dixon**: * 1959 in Sfax, Tunisia

Henry **Dreyfuss**: * 2 March 1904 in New York; † 5 October 1972 in South Pasadena, California

Marcel **Duchamp**: * 28 July 1887 in Blainville-Crevon, France; † 2 October 1968 in Neuilly-sur-Seine, France

Charles **Eames**: * 17 June 1907 in St. Louis, Missouri; † 21 August 1978 in St. Louis, Missouri

Ray **Eames**: * 15 December 1912 in Sacramento, California; † 21 August 1988 in Los Angeles

Egon **Eiermann**: * 29 September 1904 in Neuendorf, Germany; † 19 July 1970 in Baden-Baden

Yngve **Ekström**: * 16 June 1913 in Hagafors, Sweden; † 13 March 1988

Hartmut **Esslinger**: * 5 June 1944 in Beuren bei Altensteig, Germany

Otto **Firle**: * 14 October 1889 in Bonn; † 4 July 1966 in Düsseldorf

Norman **Foster**: * 1 June 1935 in Manchester

Beat **Frank**: * 1949 in Bern, Switzerland

Karin **Frankenstein**: * 1982 in Malmö, Sweden

AG (Angiolo Giuseppe) **Fronzoni**: * 15 March 1923 in Pistoia, Italy; † 2002 in Milan

Naoto **Fukasawa**: * 1956 in Yamanashi prefecture, Japan

Stefano **Giovannoni**: * 1954 in La Spezia, Italy

Michael **Graves**: * 9 July 1934 in Indianapolis

Eileen **Gray**: * 9 August 1878 in Enniscorthy, Ireland; † 31 October 1976 in Paris

Konstantin **Grcic**: * 1965 in Munich

Walter **Gropius**: * 18 May 1883 in Berlin; † 5 July 1969 in Boston

Pawel **Grunert**: * 1965 in Warsaw

Hans **Gugelot**: * 1 April 1920 in Makassar, Indonesia; † 10 September 1965 in Ulm, Germany

Zaha **Hadid**: * 31 October 1950 in Baghdad

Fritz **Haller**: * 23 October 1924 in Solothurn, Switzerland; † 15 October 2012 in Bern

Jean **Heiberg**: * 19 December 1884 in Oslo; † 27 May 1976

Robert **Heller**: * 1899; † 1973

René **Herbst**: * 1 June 1891 in Paris; † 27 August 1982 in Paris

Eva **Hesse**: * 11 January 1936 in Hamburg; † 29 May 1970 in New York

Josef **Hoffmann**: * 15 December 1870 in Pirnitz, Austria-Hungary (today Brtnice, Czech Republic); † 7 May 1956 in Vienna

Hans **Hollein**: * 30 March 1934 in Vienna

Massimo **Iosa Ghini**: * 18 June 1959 in Bologna

Arata **Isozaki**: * 23 July 1931 in Ōita, Japan

Johannes **Itten**: * 11 November 1888 in Süderen-Linden, Switzerland; † 25 May 1967 in Zurich

Jonathan **Ive**: * 27 February 1967 in London

Arne **Jacobsen**: * 11 February 1902 in Copenhagen; † 24 March 1971 in Copenhagen

Rob **Janoff**: * 1949 in Culver City, California

Charles **Jencks**: * 21 June 1939 in Baltimore, Maryland

Donald **Judd**: * 3 June 1928 in Excelsior Springs, Missouri; † 12 February 1994 in New York

Wassily **Kandinsky**: * 4 December 1866 in Moscow; † 13 December 1944 in Neuilly-sur-Seine, France

Peter **Karpf**: * 29 September 1940 in Copenhagen

Beat **Karrer**: * 1966 in Zurich

Mike **Kelley**: * 27 October 1954 in Wayne, Michigan; † 31 January 2012 in Los Angeles

Paul **Klee**: * 18 December 1879 in Münchenbuchsee, Switzerland; † 29 June 1940 in Muralto, Switzerland

Shiro **Kuramata**: * 1934 in Tokyo; † 1991 in Tokyo

Max **Lamb**: * 1980 in Cornwall, England

Le Corbusier (Charles-Édouard Jeanneret): * 6 October 1887 in La Chaux-de-Fonds, Switzerland; † 27 August 1965 in Roquebrune-Cap-Martin, France

Kwangho **Lee**: * 1967 in South Korea

Raymond **Loewy**: * 5 November 1893 in Paris; † 14 July 1986 in Monaco

Ross **Lovegrove**: * 1958 in Cardiff, Wales

Charles Rennie **Mackintosh**: * 7 June 1868 in Glasgow; † 10 December 1928 in London

Nguyen **Manh Khanh** (Quasar Khanh): * 1934 in Hanoi, Vietnam

Roberto **Marcatti**: * 6 April 1960 in Milan

Javier **Mariscal**: * February 1950 in Valencia

Alessandro **Mendini**: * 16 August 1931 in Milan

Hannes **Meyer**: * 18 November 1889 in Basel; † 19 July 1954 in Crocifisso di Lugano, Switzerland

Ludwig **Mies van der Rohe**: * 27 March 1886 in Aachen, Germany; † 17 August 1969 in Chicago

Ruben **Mochi**: * 10 December 1952

Carlo **Mollino**: * 6 May 1905 in Turin; † 27 August 1973 in Turin

William **Morris**: * 24 March 1834 in Walthamstow, England; † 3 October 1896 in London

Jasper **Morrison**: * 1959 in London

Antonio **Murado**: * 1964 in Lugo, Spain

Paola **Navone**: * 1950 in Turin

Marc **Newson**: * 20 October 1963 in Sydney

Isamu **Noguchi**: * 17 November 1904 in Los Angeles; † 30 December 1988 in New York

Eliot **Noyes**: * 12 August 1910 in Boston; † 18 July 1977 in New Canaan, Connecticut

Guido **Ooms**: * 7 July 1974 in Maasluis, Netherlands

Verner **Panton**: * 13 February 1926 in Gamtofte, Denmark; † 5 September 1998 in Copenhagen

Victor **Papanek**: * 22 November 1923 in Vienna; † 10 January 1998 in Lawrence, Kansas

Bruno **Paul**: * 19 January 1874 in Seifhennersdorf, Germany; † 17 August 1968 in Berlin

John **Pawson**: * 6 May 1949 in Halifax, Yorkshire

Joseph **Paxton**: * 3 August 1803 in Milton Bryant, Bedfordshire; † 8 June 1865 at Rockhill near Sydenham

Maurizio **Peregalli**: * 1957 in Italy

Charlotte **Perriand**: * 24 October 1903 in Paris; † 27 October 1999 in Paris

Gaetano **Pesce**: * 1939 in La Spezia, Italy

Giancarlo **Piretti**: * 1940 in Bologna

Daniela **Puppa**: * 1947 in Milan

Bernard **Quentin**: * 1923 in France

Peter **Raacke**: * 27 September 1928 in Hanau, Germany

Franco **Raggi**: * 1945 in Milan

Dieter **Rams**: * 20 May 1932 in Wiesbaden, Germany

Paul **Rand**: * 15 August 1914 in New York; † 26 November 1996 in Norwalk, Connecticut

Karim **Rashid**: * 18 September 1960 in Cairo

Tobias **Rehberger**: * 2 June 1966 in Esslingen am Neckar, Germany

Gerrit **Rietveld**: * 24 June 1888 in Utrecht, Netherlands; † 25 June 1964 in Utrecht

Edmund **Rumpler**: * 4 January 1872 in Vienna; † 7 September 1940 in Neu Tollow, Germany

John **Ruskin**: * 8 February 1819 in London; † 20 January 1900 in Brantwood, Lancashire

Eero **Saarinen**: * 20 August 1910 in Kirkkonummi, Finland; † 1 September 1961 in Ann Arbor, Michigan

Richard **Sapper**: * 30 May 1932 in Munich

Oki **Sato** (**Nendo**): * 1977 in Toronto, Canada

Paul **Schärer**: * 1933; † 2011

Gottfried **Semper**: * 29 November 1803 in Hamburg; † 15 May 1879 in Rome

Ettore **Sottsass**: * 14 September 1917 in Innsbruck, Austria; † 31 December 2007 in Milan

George James **Sowden**: * 1942 in Leeds

Mart **Stam**: * 5 August 1899 in Purmerend, Netherlands; † 23 February 1986 in Goldach, Switzerland

Philippe **Starck**: * 18 January 1949 in Paris

Walter Dorwin **Teague**: * 18 December 1883 in Decatur, Indiana; † 5 December 1960 in Flemington, New Jersey

Michael **Thonet**: * 2 July 1796 in Boppard, Germany; † 3 March 1871 in Vienna

Matteo **Thun**: * 17 June 1952 in Bolzano, Italy

Lurelle **Van Arsdale Guild**: * 1898 in Syracuse, New York; † 1985 in Darien, Connecticut

Henry **van de Velde**: * 3 April 1863 in Antwerp; † 25 October 1957 in Zurich

Theo **van Doesburg**: * 30 August 1883 in Utrecht, Netherlands; † 7 March 1931 in Davos, Switzerland

Harold **Van Doren**: * 1895 in Chicago; † 1957

Karin **van Lieshout**: * 14 September 1974 in Odiliapeel, Netherlands

Maarten **Van Severen**: * 5 June 1956 in Antwerp; † 21 February 2005 in Ghent

Robert **Venturi**: * 25 June 1925 in Philadelphia

Wilhelm **Wagenfeld**: * 15 April 1900 in Bremen; † 28 May 1990 in Stuttgart

Hans J. **Wegner**: * 2 April 1914 in Tondern, Denmark; † 26 January 2007 in Copenhagen

Robert **Wettstein**: * 1960 in Zurich

Stefan **Wewerka**: * 27 October 1928 in Magdeburg, Germany

Tapio **Wirkkala**: * 2 June 1915 in Hanko, Finland; † 19 May 1985 in Helsinki

Yanagi Sōri: * 29 June 1915 in Tokyo; † 25 December 2011 in Tokyo

LITERATURE

Antonelli, Paola, *Objects of Design from the Museum of Modern Art*, New York, London 2003

Coatts, Margot, *Pioneers of Modern Craft*, Manchester and New York 1997

Dormer, Peter, *The Illustrated Dictionary of Twentieth Century Designers*, London 1991

Droste, Magdalena, *Bauhaus: 1919–1933*, Cologne 1993

Düchting, Hajo and others, *50 Designers You Should Know*, Munich, London, New York 2012

Fiell, Charlotte and Peter, *Decorative Art: 60s*, Cologne, London 2000

Fiell, Charlotte and Peter, *Modern Furniture Classics: Since 1945*, London 1991

Fiell, Charlotte and Peter, *Design Handbook: Concepts, Materials, Styles*, Cologne, London 2006

Fiell, Charlotte and Peter, *Plastic Dreams: Synthetic Visions in Design*, London 2009

Friedewald, Boris, *Bauhaus*, Munich, London, New York 2012

Garner, Philippe, *Twentieth-Century Furniture*, London 1980

Gropius, Walter and Moholy-Nagy, László, *The New Bauhaus Books*, London 1939

Haskett, John, *Industrial Design*, London and New York 1980

Jervis, Simon, *The Penguin Dictionary of Design and Designers*, London 1984

Julier, Guy, *The Thames and Hudson Encyclopaedia of 29th Century Design and Designers*, London 1993

Kras, Reyer and other, *Icons of Design: The 20th Century*, Munich, Berlin, London, New York 2004

Marcus, George H., *Masters of Modern Design: A Critical Assessment*, New York 2005

Pevsner, Nikolaus, *Pioneers of Modern Design*, Harmondsworth 1960

Polster, Bernd and others, *The A–Z of Modern Design*, London 2006

Polster, Bernd, *Design Directory Scandinavia*, London 1999

Rippon, Max, *Sex Design*, New York 2006

Schildt, Göran, *Alvar Aalto: The Decisive Years*, New York 1986

Schönberger, Angela, *Raymond Loewy: Pioneer of American Industrial Design*, Munich, London 1990

Siebenbrodt, Michael, *Bauhaus Weimar: Designs for the Future*, Ostfildern 2000

Strasser, Josef, *50 Bauhaus Icons You Should Know*, Munich, Berlin, London, New York 2009

Vegesack, Alexander von, *Thonet: Classic Furniture in Bent Wood and Tubular Steel*, London 1996

Wingler, Hans M., *The Bauhaus: Weimar, Dessau, Berlin, Chicago*, Cambridge, MA, 1969

Woodham, Jonathan M., *A Dictionary of Modern Design*, Oxford 2004

INDEX

Numbers in *italics* refer to images.

PHOTO CREDITS

Tapio Wirkkala Rut Bryk Foundation: Frontispiece; © Vitra/Hans Hansen: p. 6; Cassina, Mailand/Mario Carrieri: p. 8; akg-images: pp. 9, 11, 178; IAM/akg-images: p. 13; Magnus Manske: p. 14; © Vitra (www.vitra.com): pp. 17, 22, 78, 96, 100, 136, 138,140; Thonet GmbH: pp. 18, 20, 24/25, 42, 45, 68, 70 right, 92 right; Artek: pp. 21, 74, 75, 84 above; © Fritz Hansen: p. 23; © Voxia: p. 26; Beat Frank: p. 27; Hans Engels: p. 28; akg-images/Bildarchiv Monheim: p. 30; Bauhaus-Archiv, Berlin: pp. 31, 35; S. 32 Photo: Horst Wedemeyer/Archive Prestel Verlag; Die Neue Sammlung. The International Design Museum, Munich (Photos: A. Laurenzo): pp. 36, 46, 131; Jacek Marczewski © The Museum of Modern Art, New York: pp. 38/39; Vitra Design Museum, Weil am Rhein: pp. 40, 110, 114, 185; © Peter Strobel: p. 44; Alessi: pp. 48, 49, 51; Raymond Loewy Foundation, Hamburg: pp. 52, 58; Courtesy of Mark Newson Limited: p. 59; © AEG Haustechnik: p. 60; Braun, Kronberg: p. 62; © Lufthansa: p. 64; ERCO GmbH: p. 65; © 2013 Apple Inc.: pp. 66, 67; TECTA, Lauenförde: pp. 70 left, 71, 73; Konstantin Grcic Industrial Design: pp. 76/77; Vitra Collections AG: pp. 80/81; Tapio Wirkkala Rut Bryk Foundation: pp. 84 below, 85; Wilhelm Schimmel Pianofortefabrik GmbH: p. 86; Terry Dwan: p. 87; © Zanotta Spa: pp. 89, 119; Inter IKEA Systems B.V.: pp. 90, 92 left, 93, 94, 95; Sepha Wouda: p. 98; © Muji: p. 99; Holger Ellgaard: p. 103; Tupperware, Frankfurt/Main: p. 105; Verner Panton Design, Bern: pp. 106/107, 118; Ron Arad Associates: p. 108; © Philippe Starck: pp. 109 left, 124, 169; © Lovegrove: p. 109 right; Superstudio: p. 112; © ADELTA: p. 115; Ignazia Favata/Studio Joe Colombo, Milano: pp. 116/117; Studio Ettore Sottsass srl: p. 120; Atelier Mendini: pp. 122, 123; Poltronova Italy: p. 127; Cap Design Spa: pp. 128, 135; © Zeus, Milano: pp. 132, 134; Tom Vack, München © Ingo Maurer GmbH, München: p. 139; © Shigeru Ban Architects: p. 142; © Nendo: p. 143; Artemide: p. 144; akg-images/Paul Almasy: p. 147; Alberto Fioravanti: p. 148; Aldo Ballo: p. 149; Zaha Hadid Architects: pp. 150/151; © Luis Calazans: p. 152; Pilot Pen GmbH: p. 154; Marek Fijalkowski: pp. 156/157; Dyson GmbH: p. 159; Woodnotes Oy (Ltd.): pp. 160, 161; © OOOMS (www.oooms.nl): pp. 162, 166; b.d barcelona design: p. 164; © REHHAB: p. 165; Suck UK Ltd.: p. 168; Walter Gumiero: p. 173; Hans Hansen/FSB: p. 174; Studio Morrison: pp. 175, 176; © Fernando Laszlo: p. 181; Droog Design: p. 182; Kevin Noble © The Noguchi Museum, New York: p. 184; © Tobias Rehberger: pp. 186/187

IMPRINT

© Prestel Verlag, Munich · London · New York, 2013

© for the works reproduced is held by the artists, their heirs or assigns, with the exception of: Alvar Aalto with © VG Bild-Kunst, Bonn 2013; Eero Aarnio with © Eero Aarnio; Otl Aicher with Florian Aicher; Ron Arad with © Ron Arad; Shigeru Ban © Shigeru Ban Architects; Mario Botta with © Mario Botta; Fernando and Humberto Campana with © Fernando and Humberto Campana; Luigi Colani with © Luigi Colani; Joe Colombo with © Studio Joe Colombo, Milano; Le Corbusier © FLC / VG Bild-Kunst, Bonn 2013; Mia Cullin with © Mia Cullin; Marcel Duchamp with © Succession Marcel Duchamp / VG Bild-Kunst, Bonn 2013; Terry Dwan with © Terry Dwan; Charles and Ray Eames with © Eames Foundation; Norman Foster with © Norman Foster; Beat Frank with © Beat Frank; Frank Gehry with © Frank Gehry; Michael Graves with © Michael Graves; Konstantin Grcic © with Konstantin Grcic; Walter Gropius with © VG Bild-Kunst, Bonn 2013; Pawel Grunert with © Pawel Grunert; Zaha Hadid with © Zaha Hadid; Hans Hollein with © Hans Hollein; Pierre Jeanneret with © VG Bild-Kunst, Bonn 2013; Donald Judd with © Judd Foundation; Peter Karpf with © Peter Karpf; Raymond Loewy with © Raymond Loewy Foundation; Ross Lovegrove with © Ross Lovegrove; Ingo Maurer with © Ingo Maurer; Alessandro Mendini with © Alessandro Mendini; Ludwig Mies van der Rohe with © VG Bild-Kunst, Bonn 2012; Jasper Morrison with © Jasper Morrison; Nendo with © Nendo; Marc Newson with © Marc Newson; Isamu Noguchi © The Isamu Noguchi Foundation and Garden Museum / VG Bild-Kunst, Bonn 2012; Verner Panton with © Verner Panton Design, Basel; Maurizio Peregalli with © Maurizio Peregalli; Charlotte Perriand with © VG Bild-Kunst, Bonn 2012; Alexander Reh with © Alexander Reh; Tobias Rehberger with © Tobias Rehberger; Ettore Sottsass with © Studio Ettore Sottsass; Philippe Starck with © Philippe Starck; Stefan Wewerka with © Stefan Wewerka; Tapio Wirkkala with © Tapio Wirkkala Rut Bryk-Foundation

Front cover: Arne Jacobsen, *Ant* chairs, see p. 23
Back cover: (from left to right): Michael Thonet, *No. 14*, see p. 92; Dieter Rams, *Sixtant SM 31*, see p. 62; Philippe Starck, *Juicy Salif*, see p. 51
Frontispiece: Tapio Wirkkala, *Kantarelli* vase, see p. 85

Prestel Verlag, Munich
A member of Verlagsgruppe Random House GmbH

Prestel Verlag
Neumarkter Strasse 28
81673 Munich
Tel. +49 (0)89 4136-0
Fax +49 (0)89 4136-2335
www.prestel.de

Prestel Publishing Ltd.
14–17 Wells Street
London W1T 3PD
Tel. +44 (0)20 7323-5004
Fax +44 (0)20 7636-8004
www.prestel.com

Prestel Publishing
900 Broadway, Suite 603
New York, NY 10003
Tel. +1 (212) 995-2720
Fax +1 (212) 995-2733
www.prestel.com

Library of Congress Control Number: 2013934194; British Library Cataloguing-in-Publication Data: a catalogue record for this book is available from the British Library; Deutsche Nationalbibliothek holds a record of this publication in the Deutsche Nationalbibliografie; detailed bibliographical data can be found under: http://www.dnb.de

Prestel books are available worldwide. Please contact your nearest bookseller or one of the above addresses for information concerning your local distributor.

„CH" at the end of the text entries refers to the co-author Claudia Hellmann.

Translated by: Jane Michael, Munich
Editorial direction: Claudia Stäuble and Julie Kiefer
Copyedited by: Chris Murray
Picture editor: Andrea Weißenbach, Utting am Ammersee
Index and timelines: Franziska Stegmann, Munich
Cover design: Joana Niemeyer., April
Design concept: LIQUID, Agentur für Gestaltung, Augsburg
Layout: Wolfram Söll, Munich
Production: René Fink
Origination: ReproLine Mediateam, Munich
Printing and binding: Druckerei Uhl GmbH & Co. KG, Radolfzell

Printed in Germany

MIX
Paper from responsible sources
FSC® C004229
www.fsc.org

Verlagsgruppe Random House FSC® N001967
The FSC®-certified paper *Hello Fat matt*
was supplied by Deutsche Papier

ISBN 978-3-7913-4788-2